CONTENTS

Hear the Song

What Is A Friend

A Mother's Love

Australia

Time Is Ticking

The Cycle

Days That Count

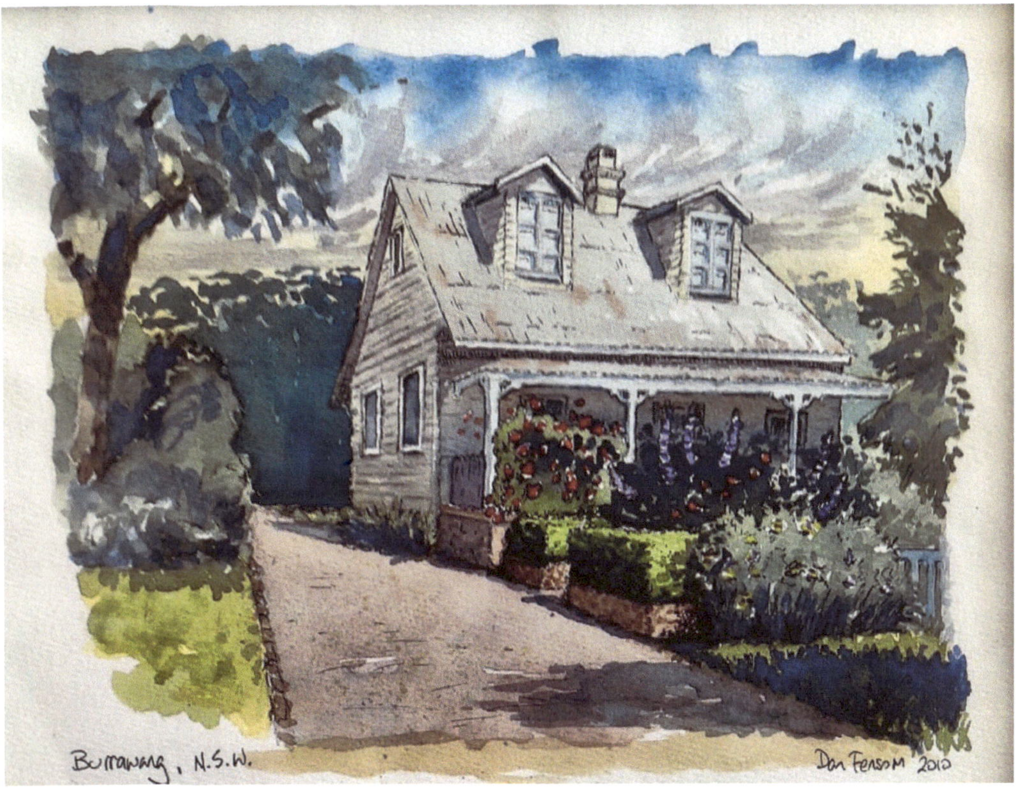

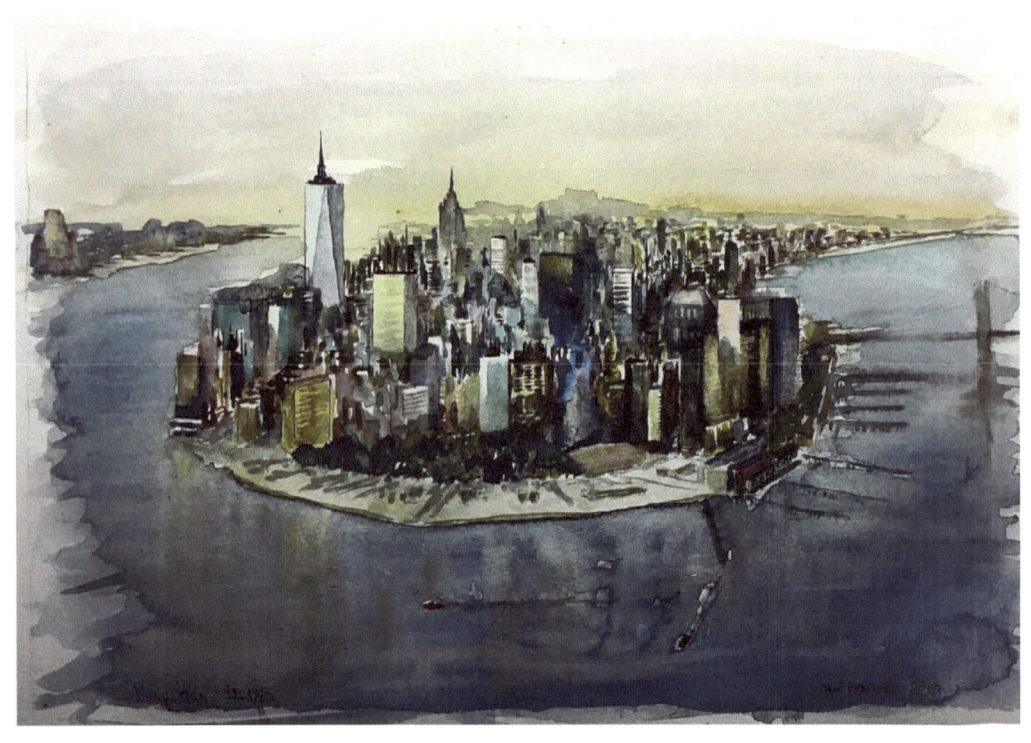

HEAR THE SONG

Woke again to nothing new

Another day to rush on through

Feet beating ground like sticks on drums

The thumping made my mind go numb

But life was changed for me today
By a man who blocked my way

I was about to rush on by
But saw a sparkle in his eye

I asked him why he moved so slow
Did he have no place to go?

His answer, well it shot me through
And changed my narrow point of view

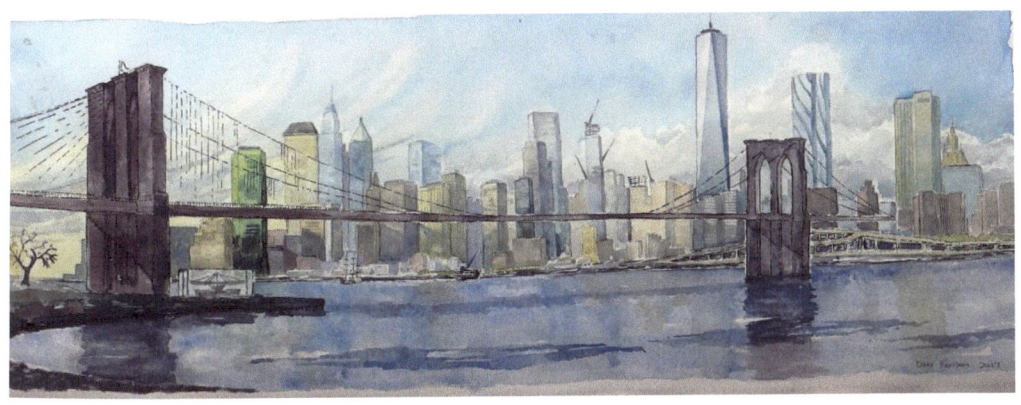

The words he said, I'll try to say
To them please, attention pay…

"A running man gets nowhere fast

Chases wind then breathes his last

The road he runs with gold he'll pave

Then speeds his way right to his grave

He cannot hear life's gentle song

Or learn the words and sing along

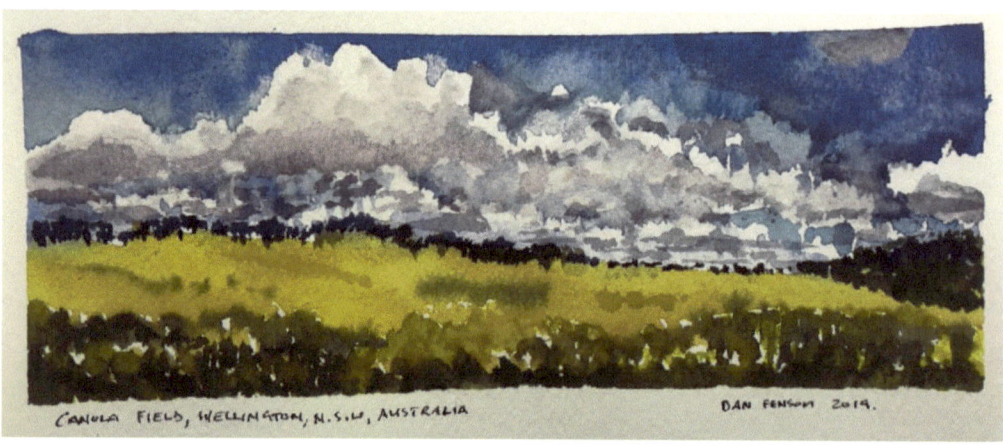

He has no time, he must move fast

Then learns too late, the best is past

Once like you, I also ran

But made a choice to change that man

Now I'm slow I have the chance

To hear the tune and share the dance

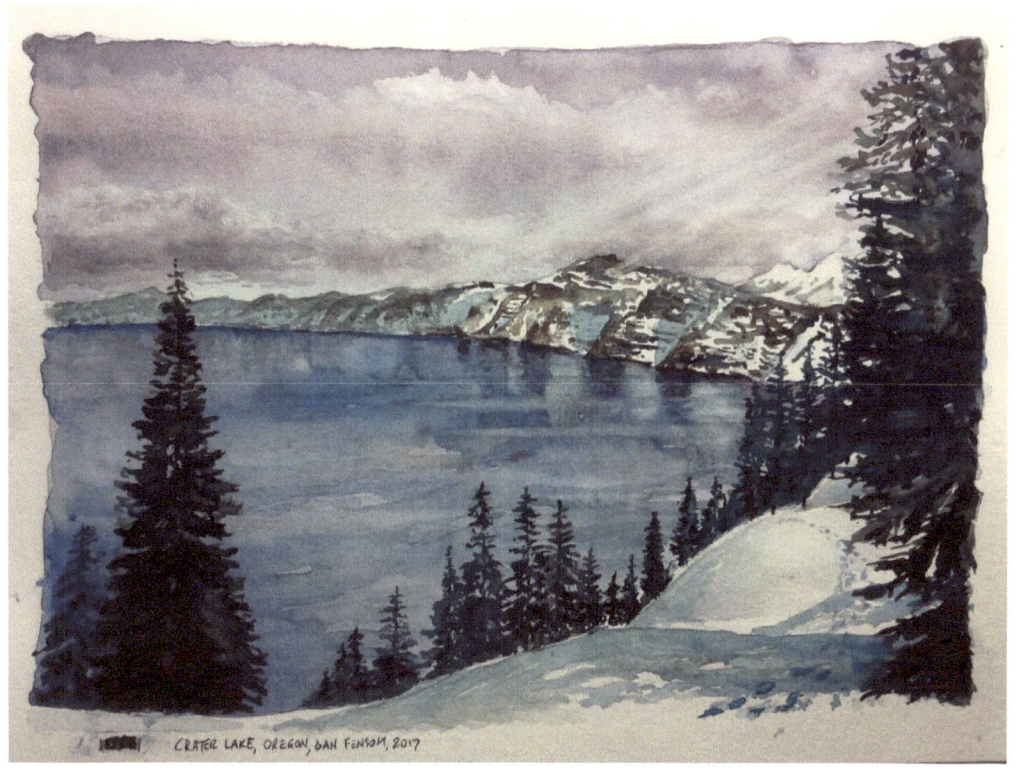

Slow your pace, you'll hear it too

An orchestra with songs for you

Strings you'll hear in wind in trees

Percussion in the blowing leaves

The horns will blast as egrets call

A tweeting flute from wrens so small

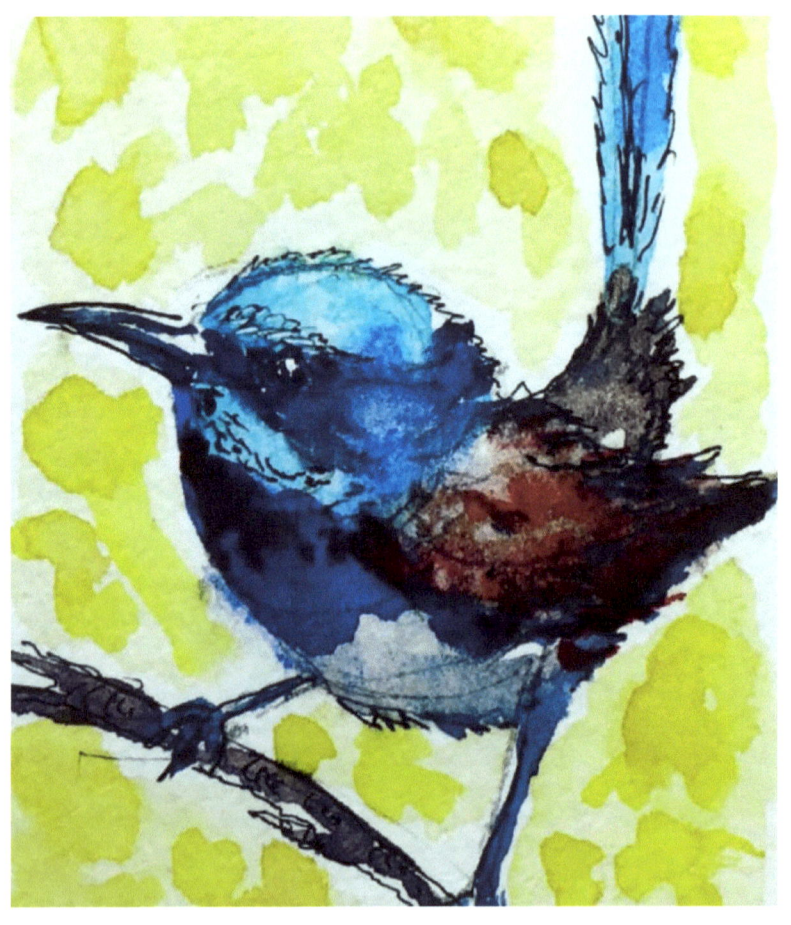

The choir's voice in heads of grain

A gentle drum in drops of rain"

The man paused there, then what he said

Changed the path on which I tread.

"Who made the players and the songs?

To whom do all these things belong?

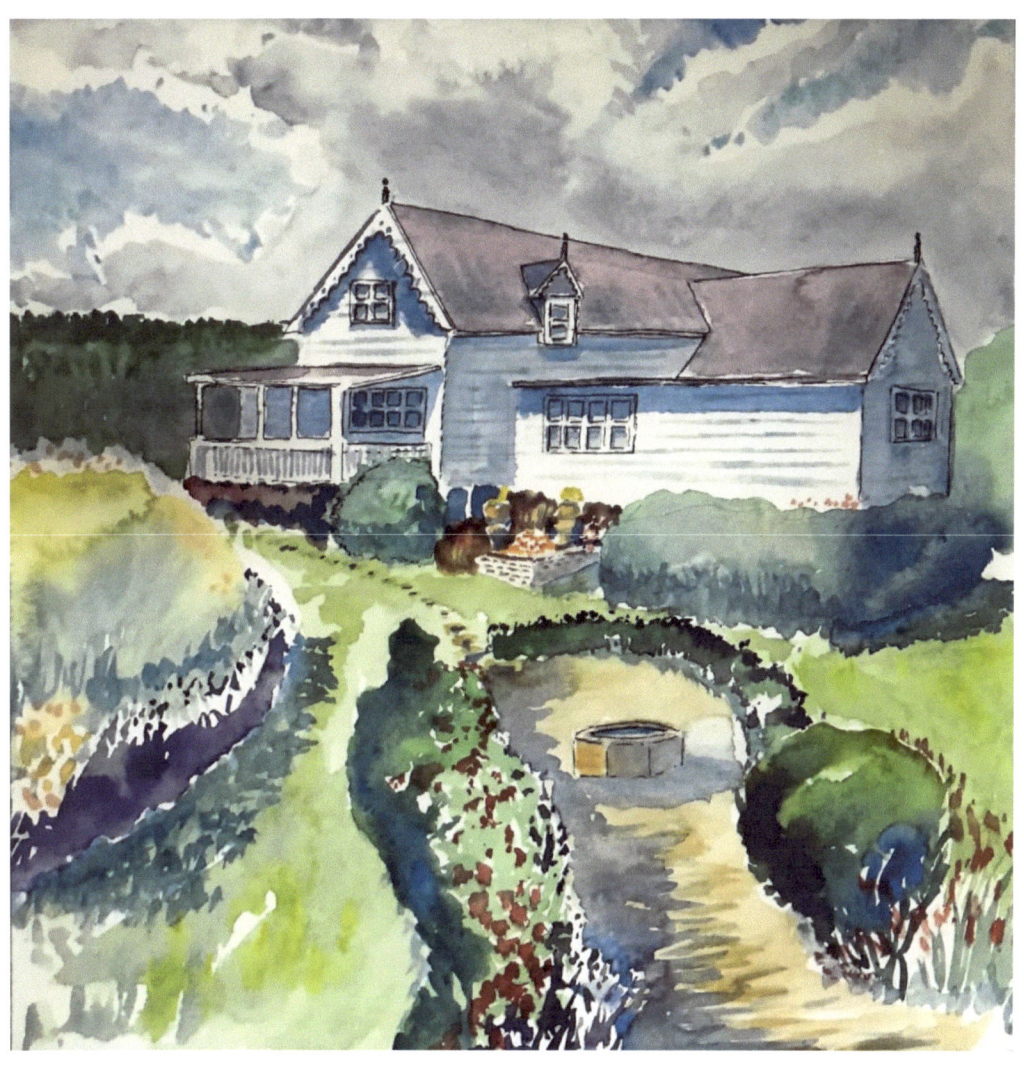

These natural tunes to us appeal

To draw us close and see what's real

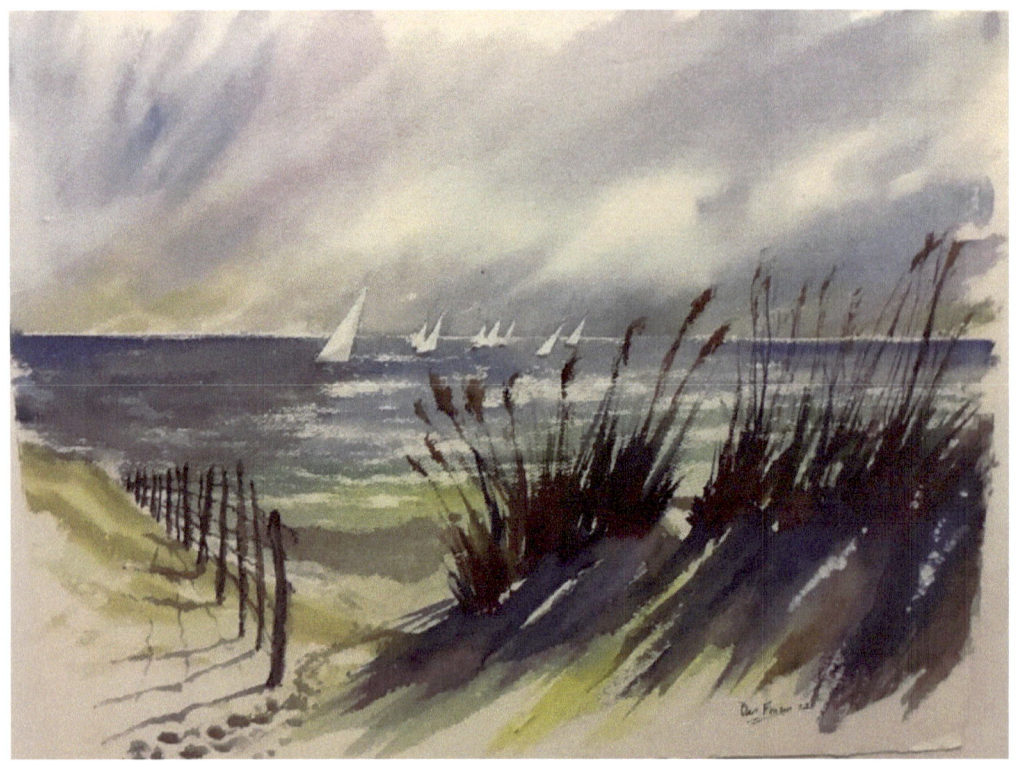

This music's made to give us hope

And with our many troubles cope.

The sacred songs that they inspire

Are gifts to us to lift us higher

The outer man may waste away

The inner man's renewed each day

So slow your pace, and linger long

Learn to live—Hear the song"

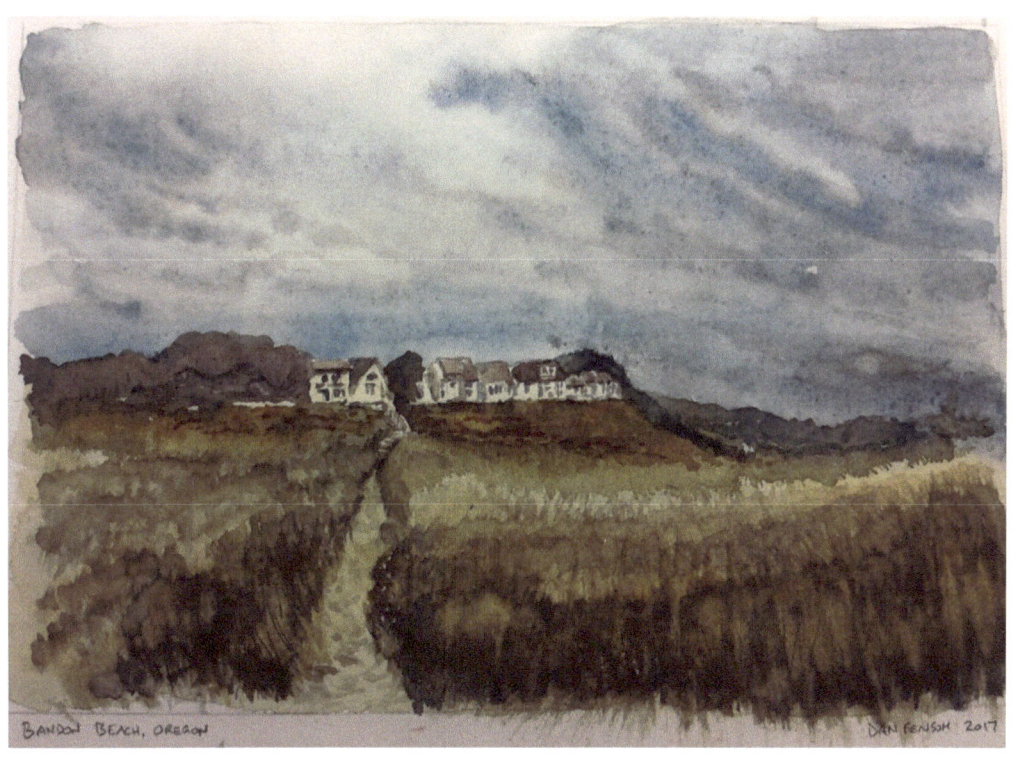

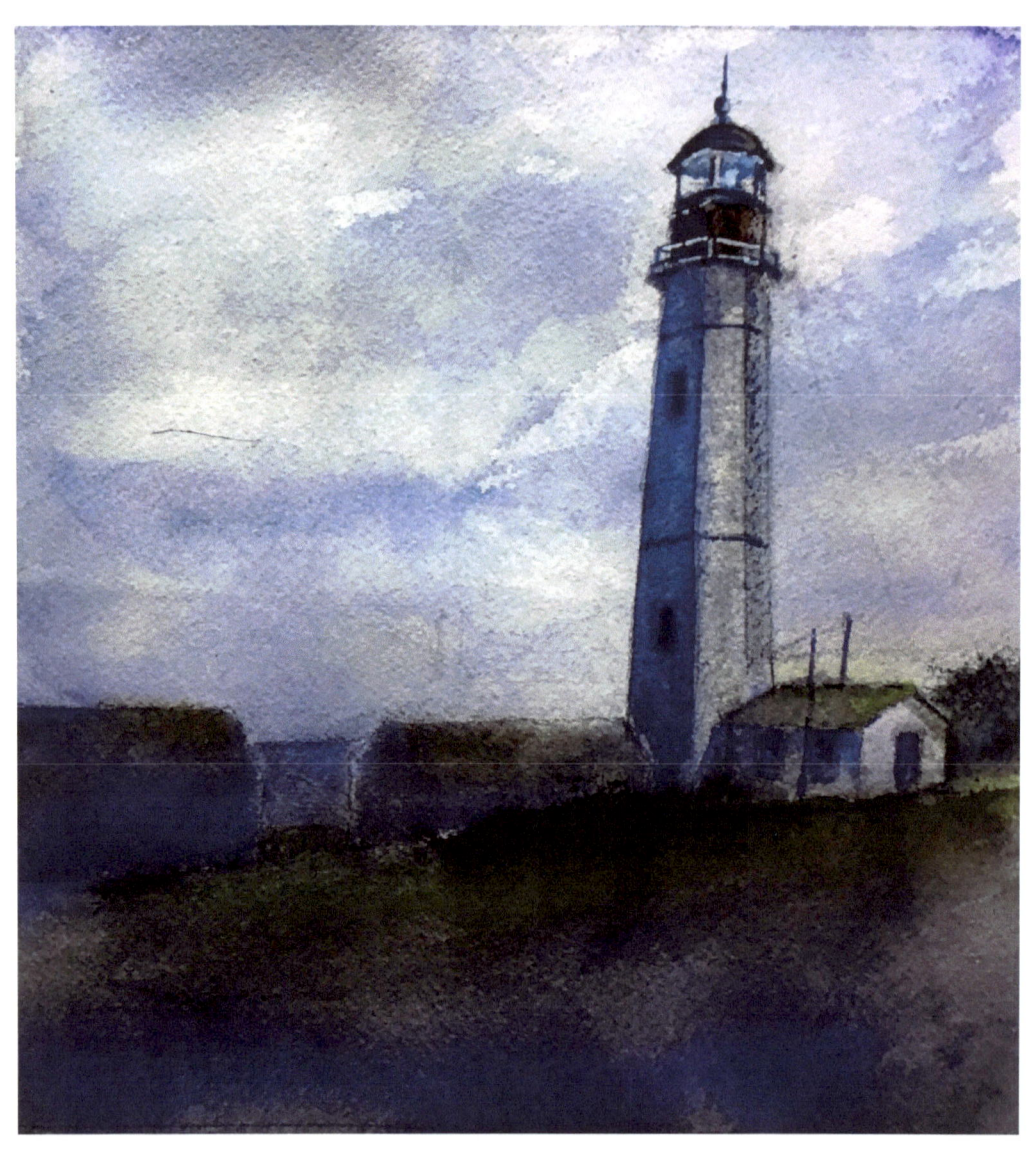

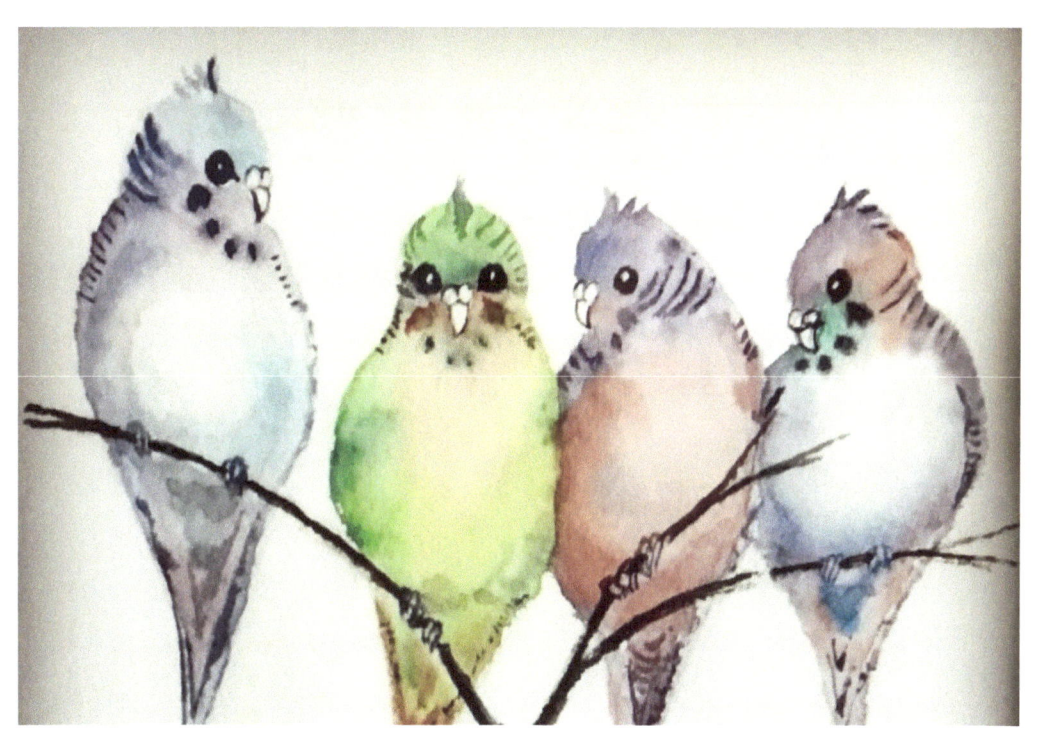

WHAT IS A FRIEND?

A friend likes what you like

Not because you're friends

But because you're right

If you're wrong

She'll be the first to tell you

But if you're wrong for good reason

She'll defend you like the error was her own

A friend doesn't worry about the odds

Or about how odd you may be

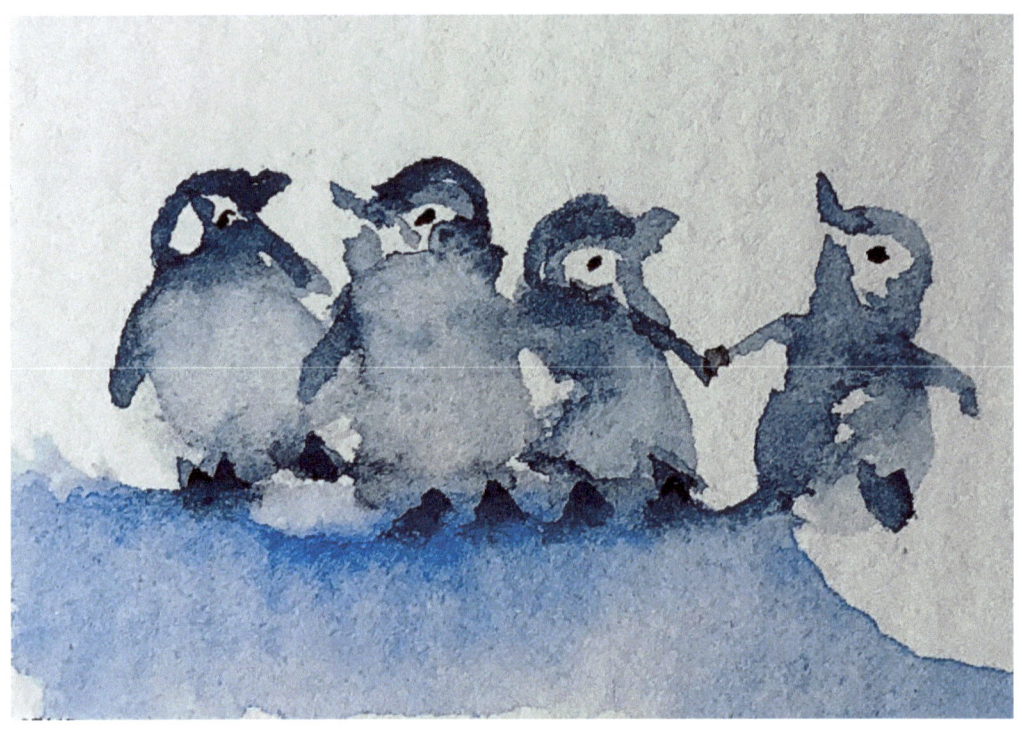

According to her reckoning

You against the world is an even match

And the two of you together can conquer all

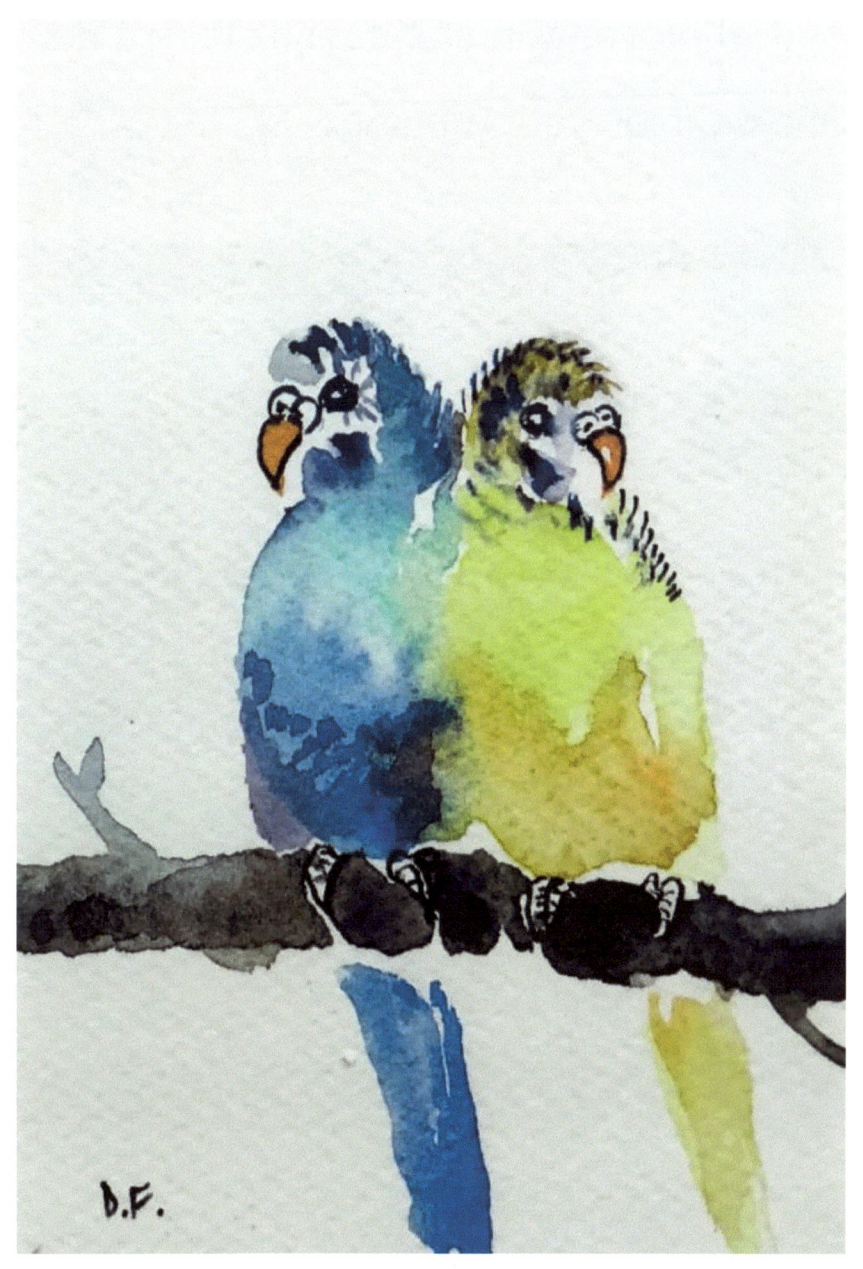

A friend feels your pain

Sometimes more than you do

And in the process

She more than halves it

And when you win she doesn't take a tax

She doubles your winning

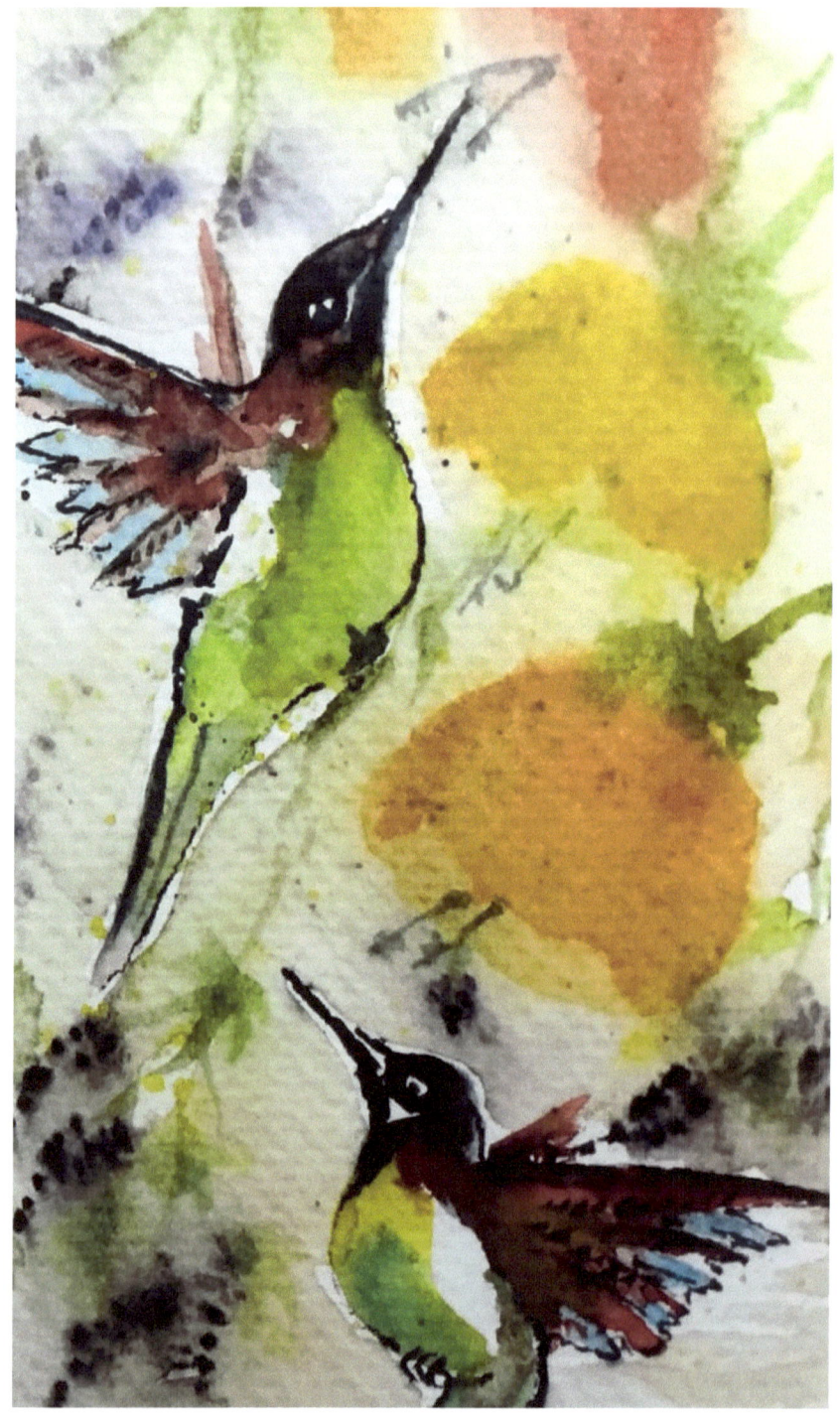

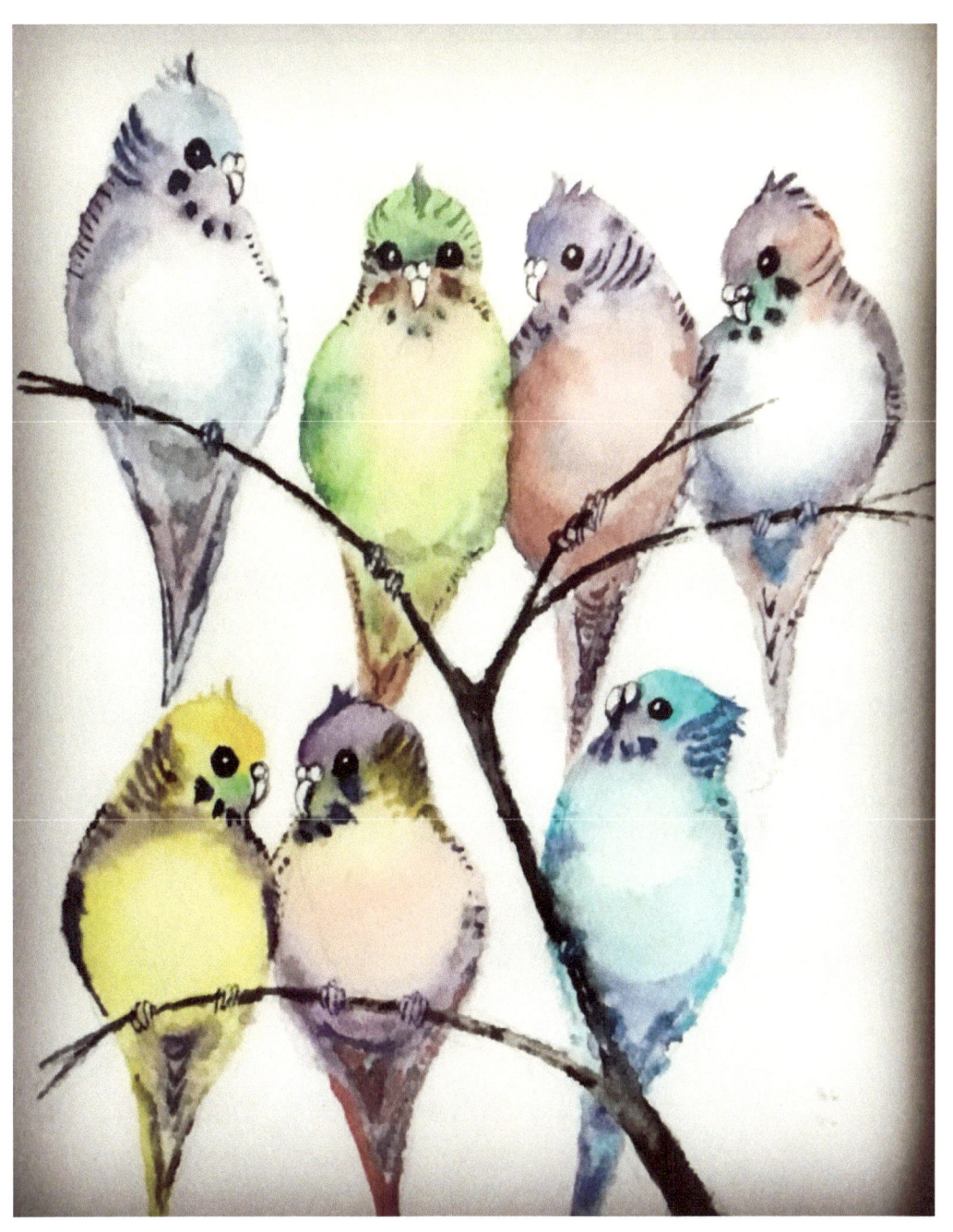

A friend is not owned or even borrowed;

She is shared

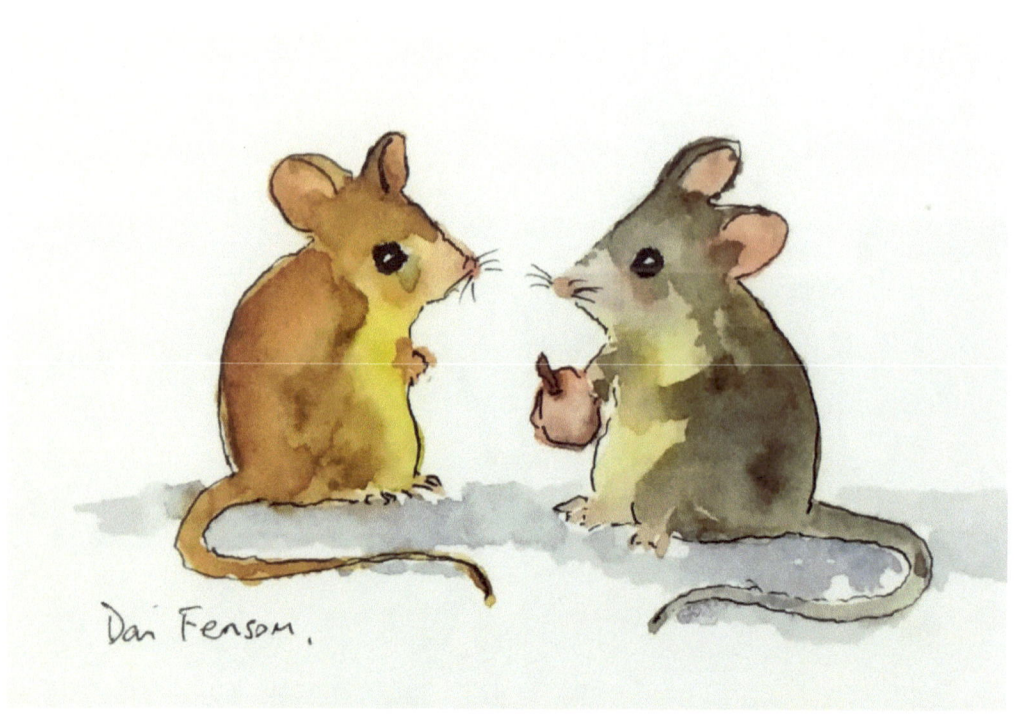

And in the sharing increases in value

She makes you richer with her company

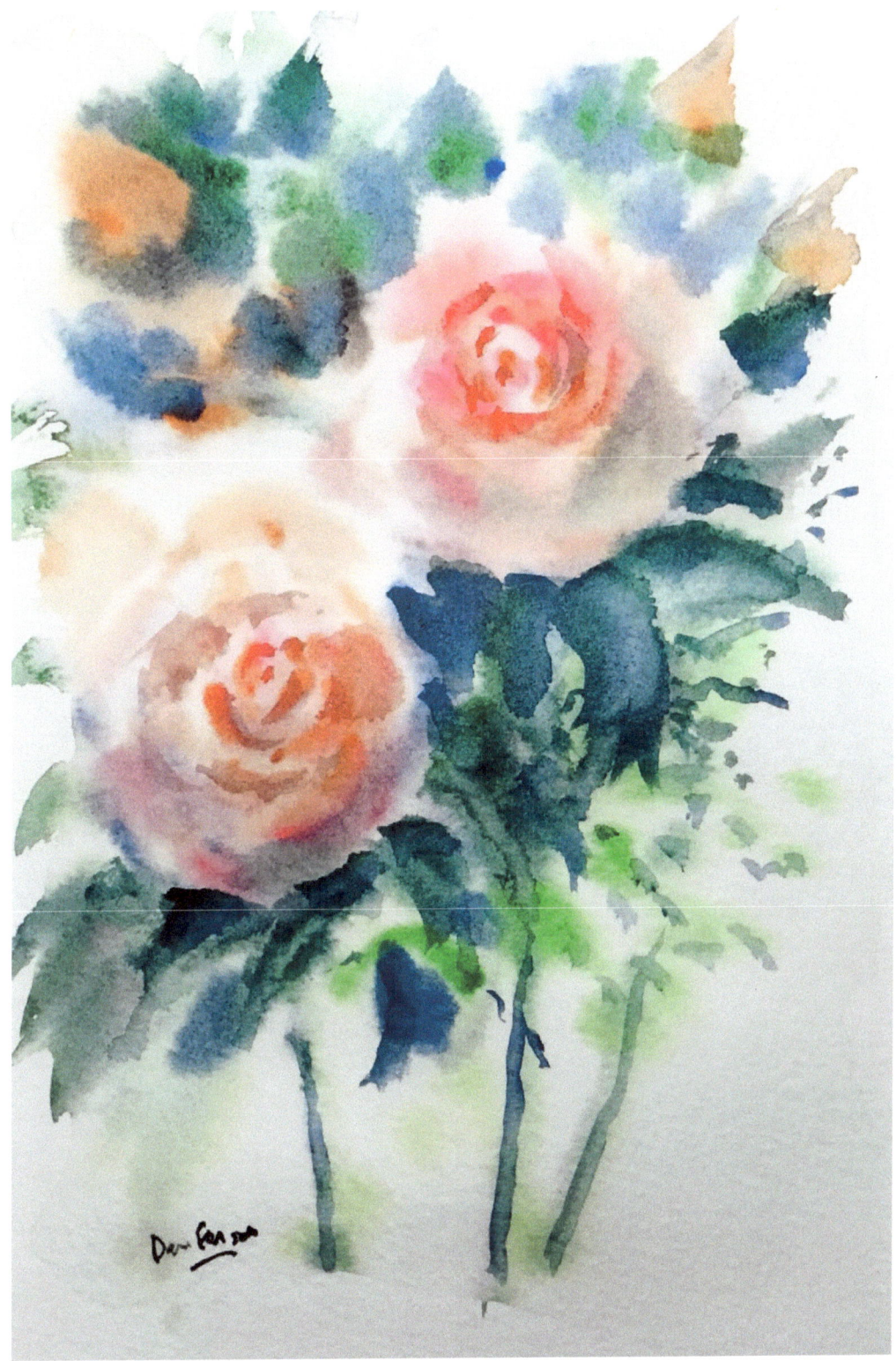

A MOTHER'S LOVE

Seas so deep and mountains high

All those stars up in the sky

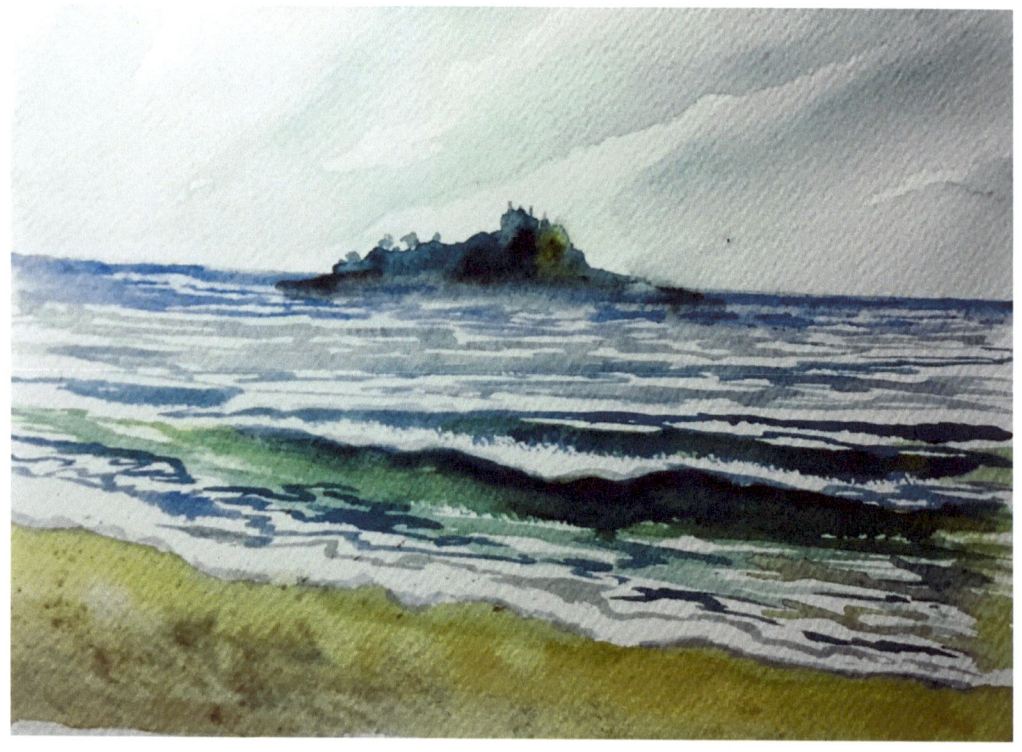

Seems these things will never end

Seems on these you can depend

But seas will dry and hills decay

Stars will burst and fade away

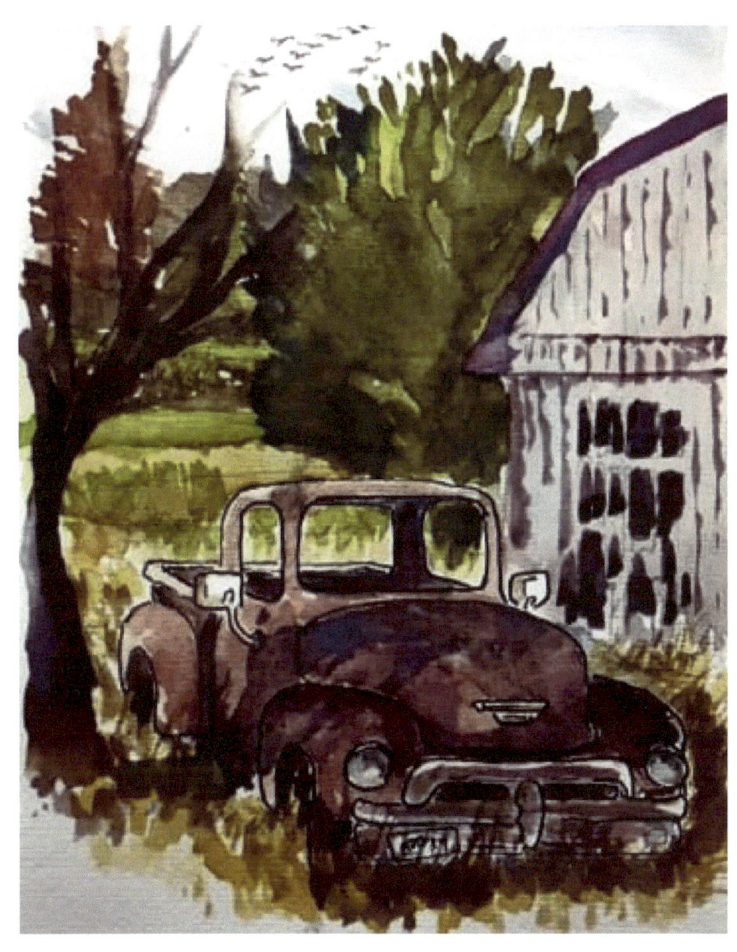

Few are things that will not rust

Even diamonds turn to dust

There is one bond, forever lasts

Strength retains though time has past

This potent force is from above

The precious gift…

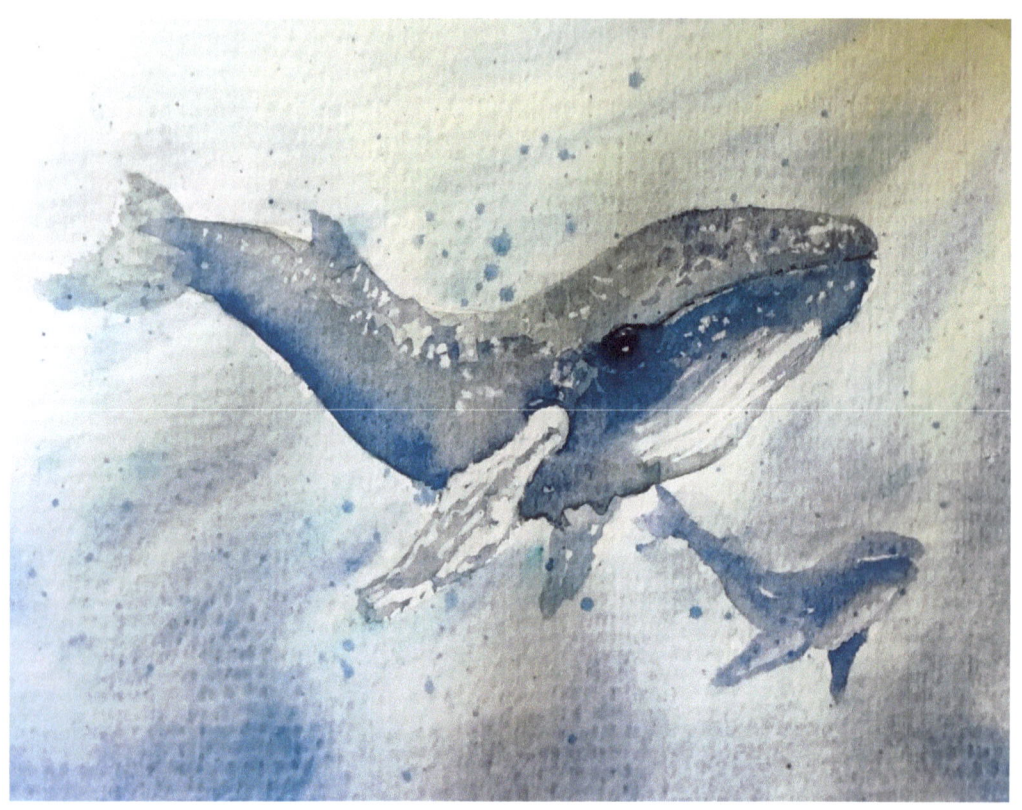

a mother's love

As I grew and took my stand

She'd guide me with her gentle hand

A hand that soothed my childish fears

A hand now bent by weight of years

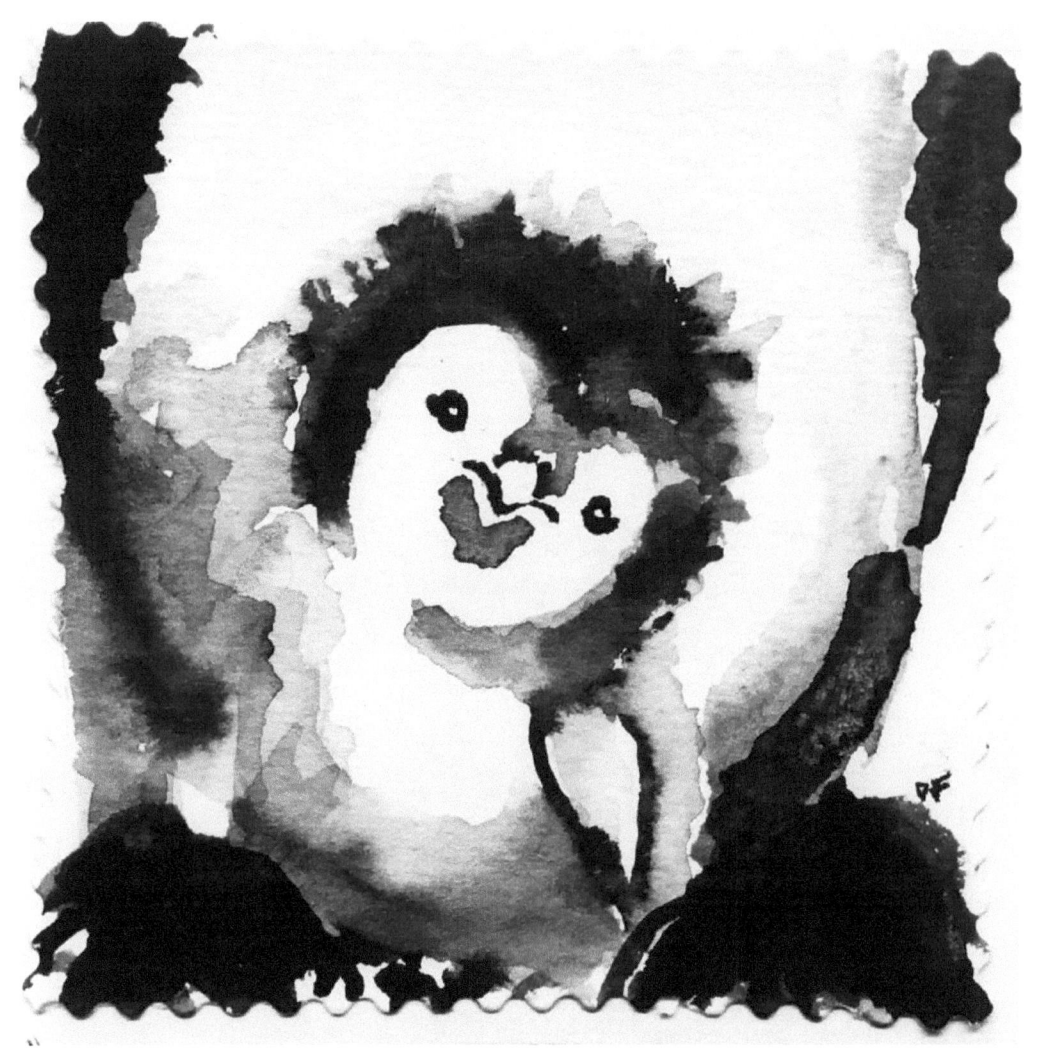

I took my mother's care each day

But seldom words of thanks I'd say

Still she gave without regret

A lesson learned I won't forget!

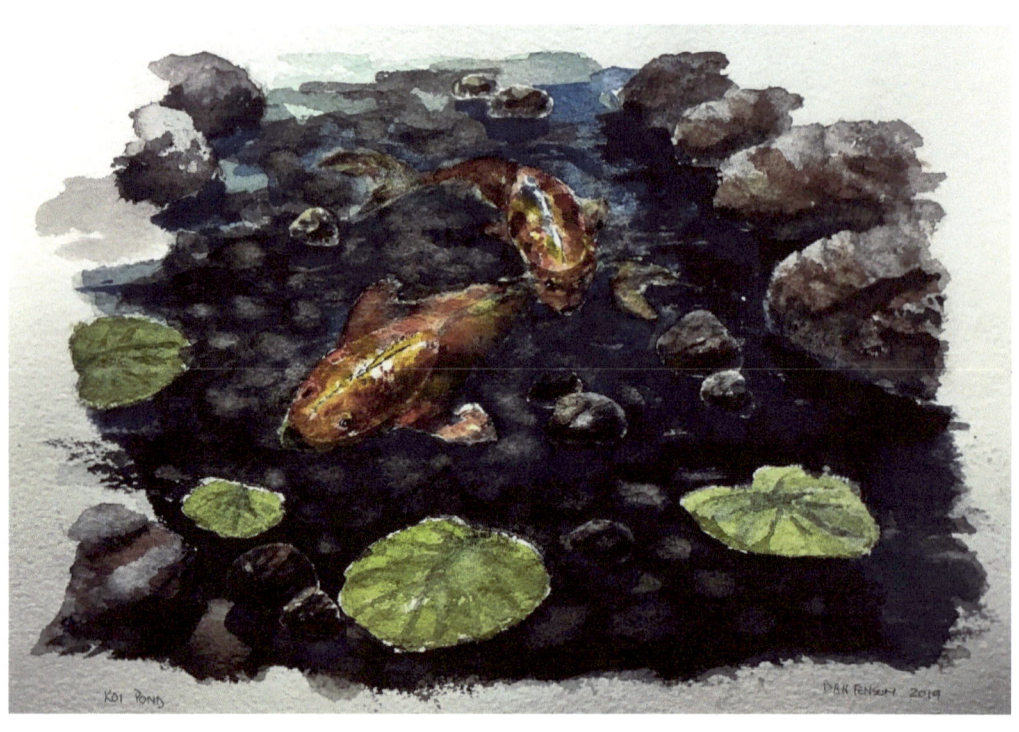

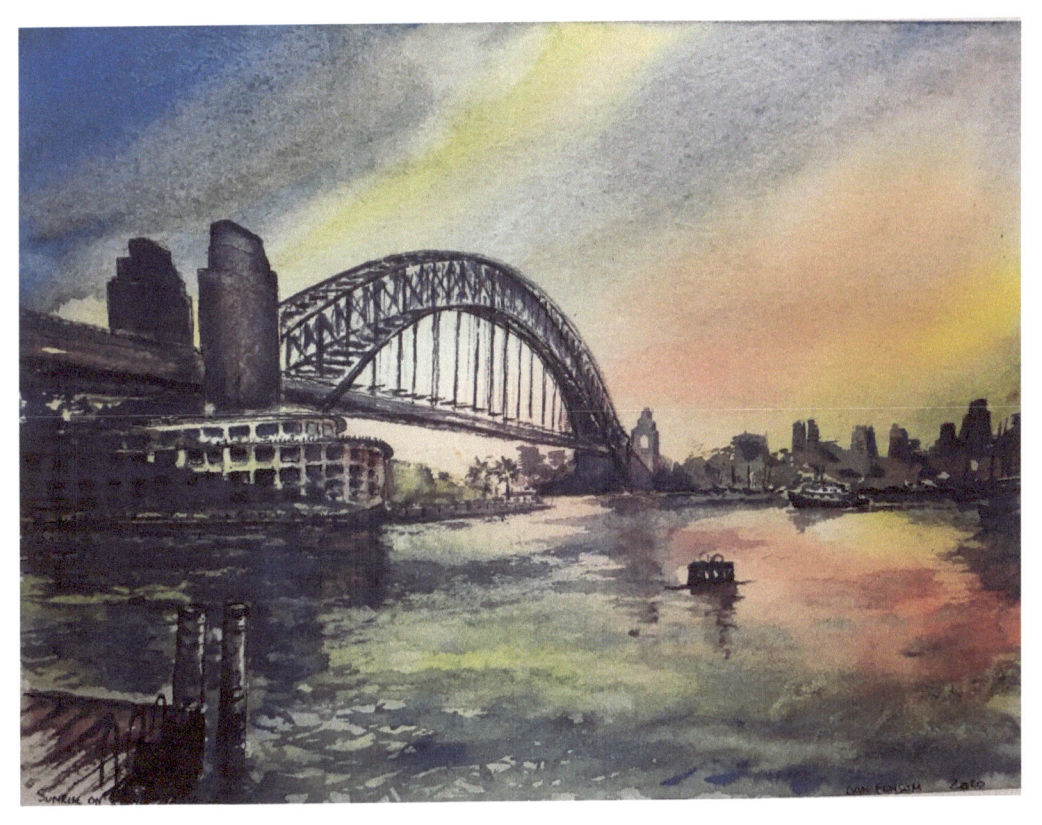

AUSTRALIA

Days are long

Nights are bright

Sprinkled with

A million lights

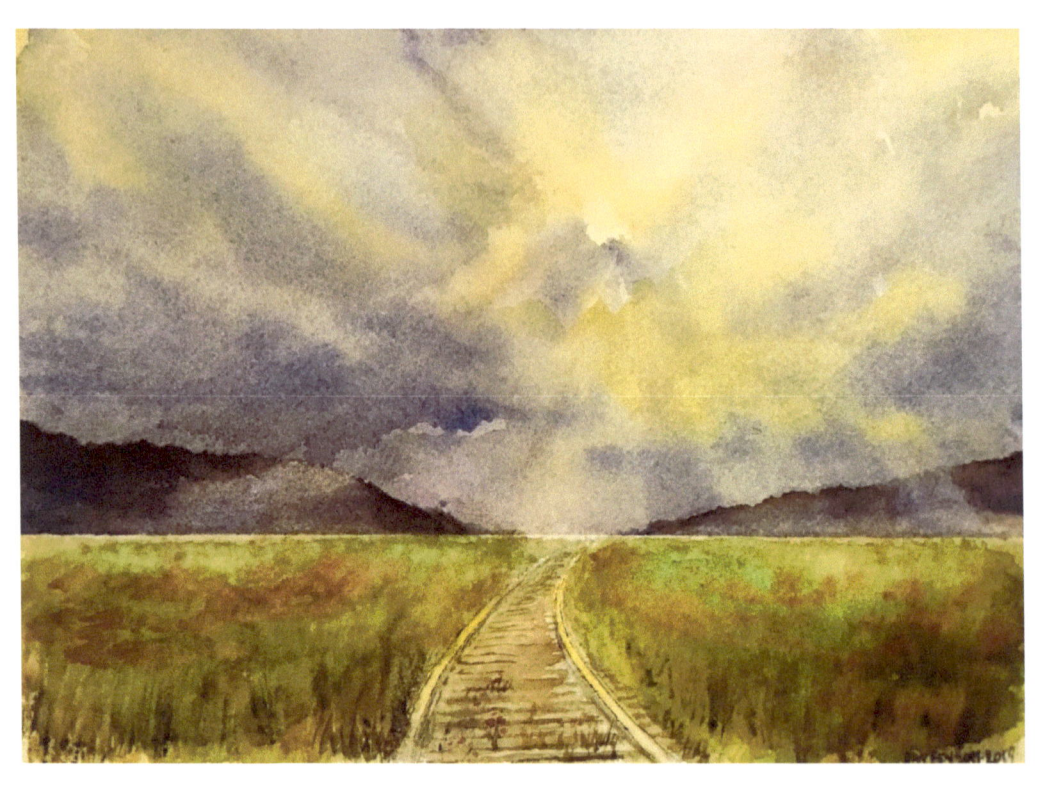

Earth is hard

But water-worn

Mountains knarled

By time are torn

Trees are tired

Leaves droop n sag

They burst on fire

Like an oily rag

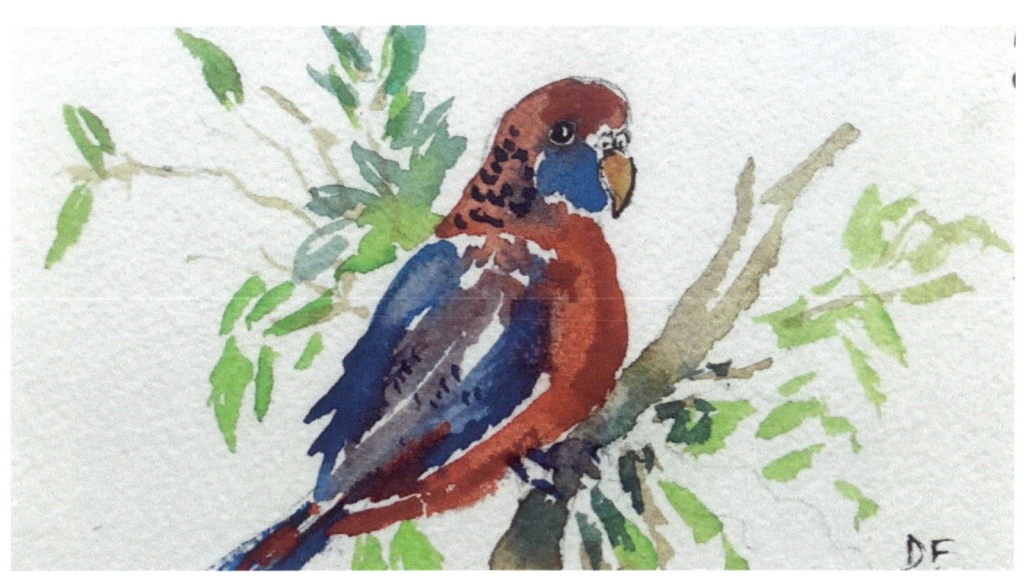

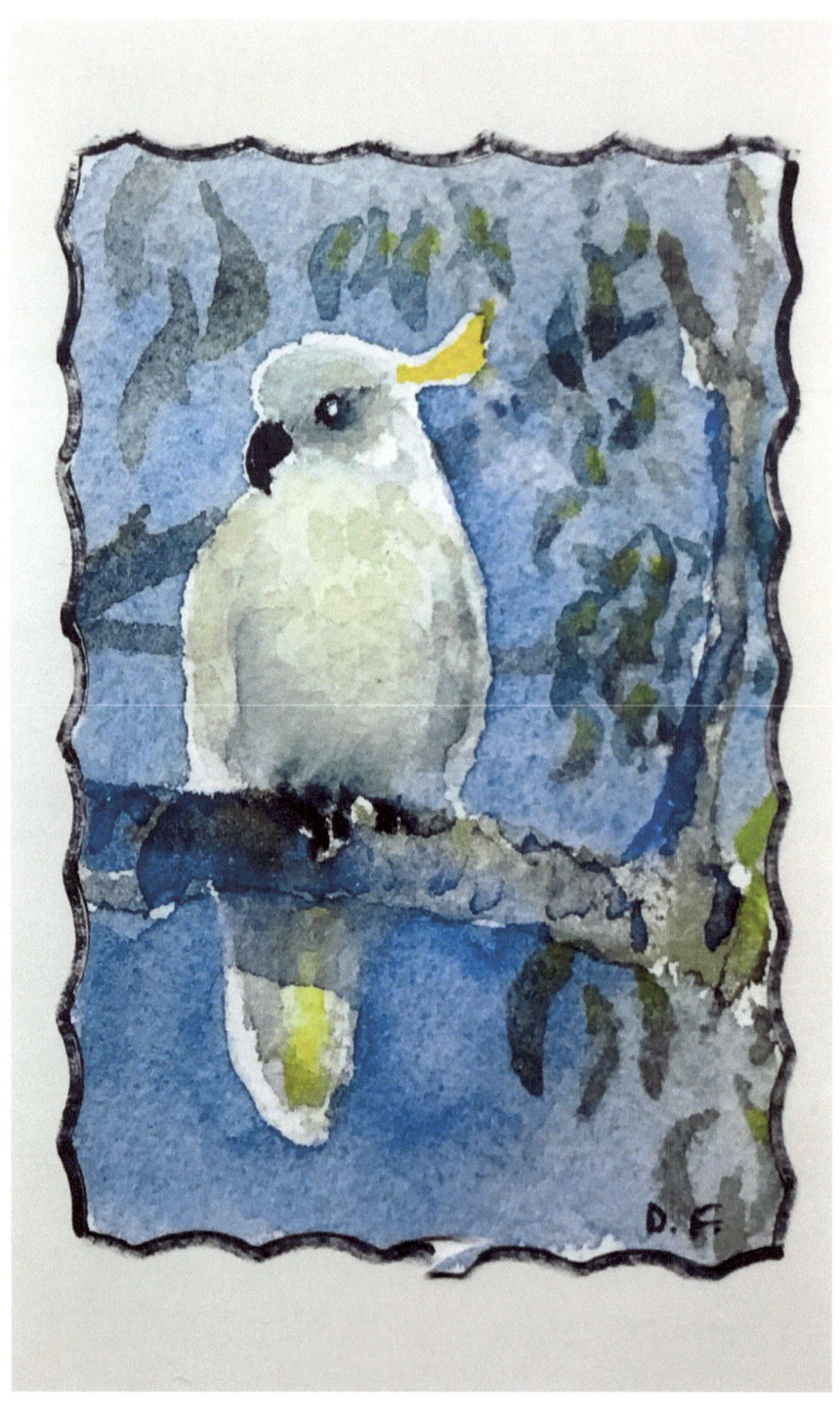

Dingoes howl

Cockies screech

Galahs complain

In mournful speech

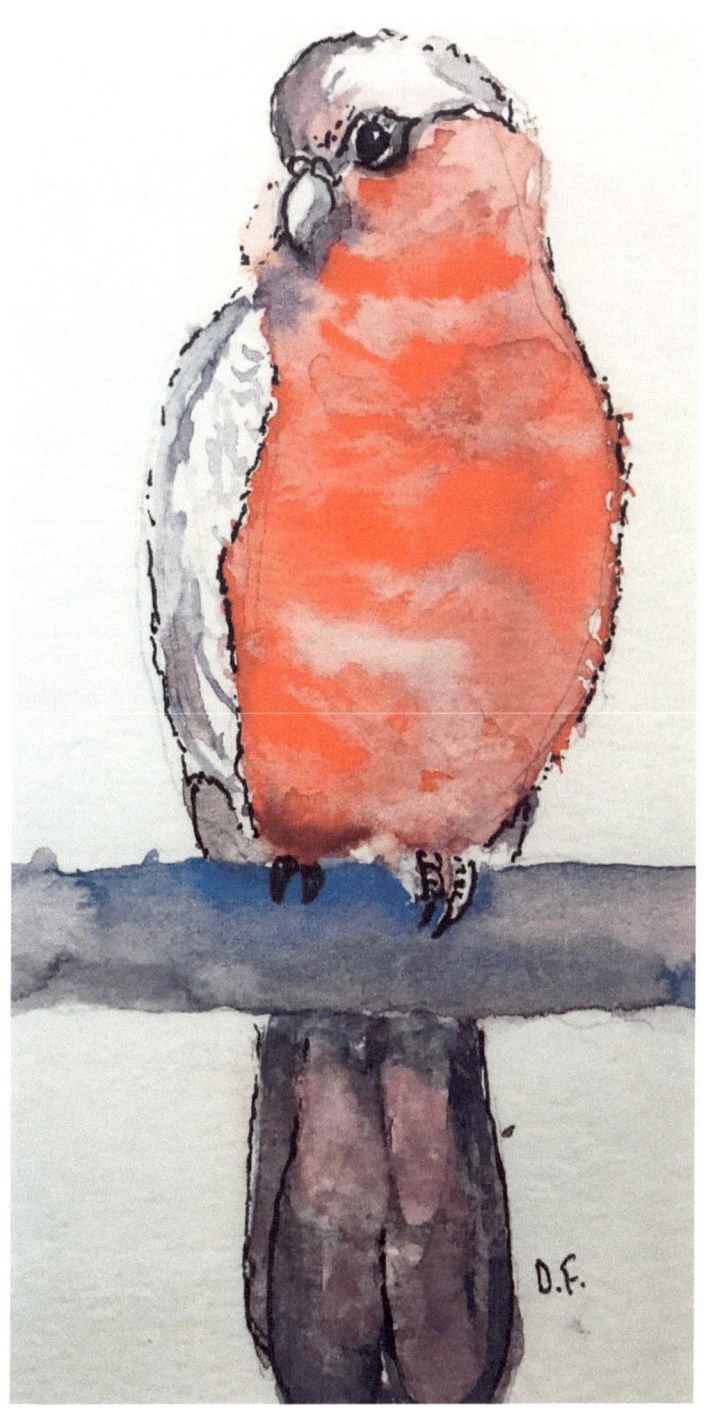

Roos they bounce

High as they can

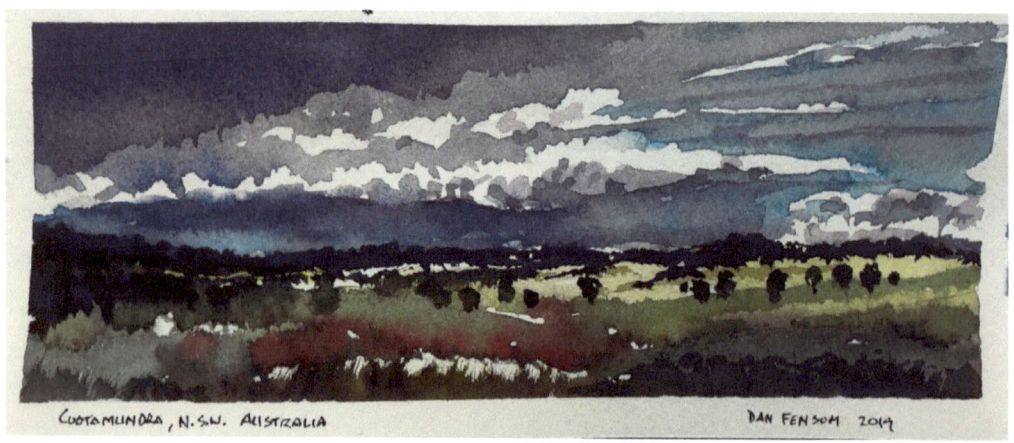

Like popping corn

In a frying pan

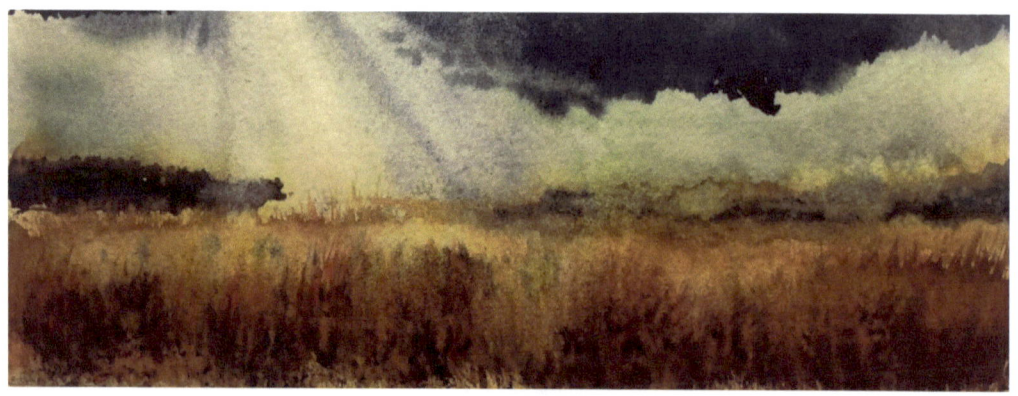

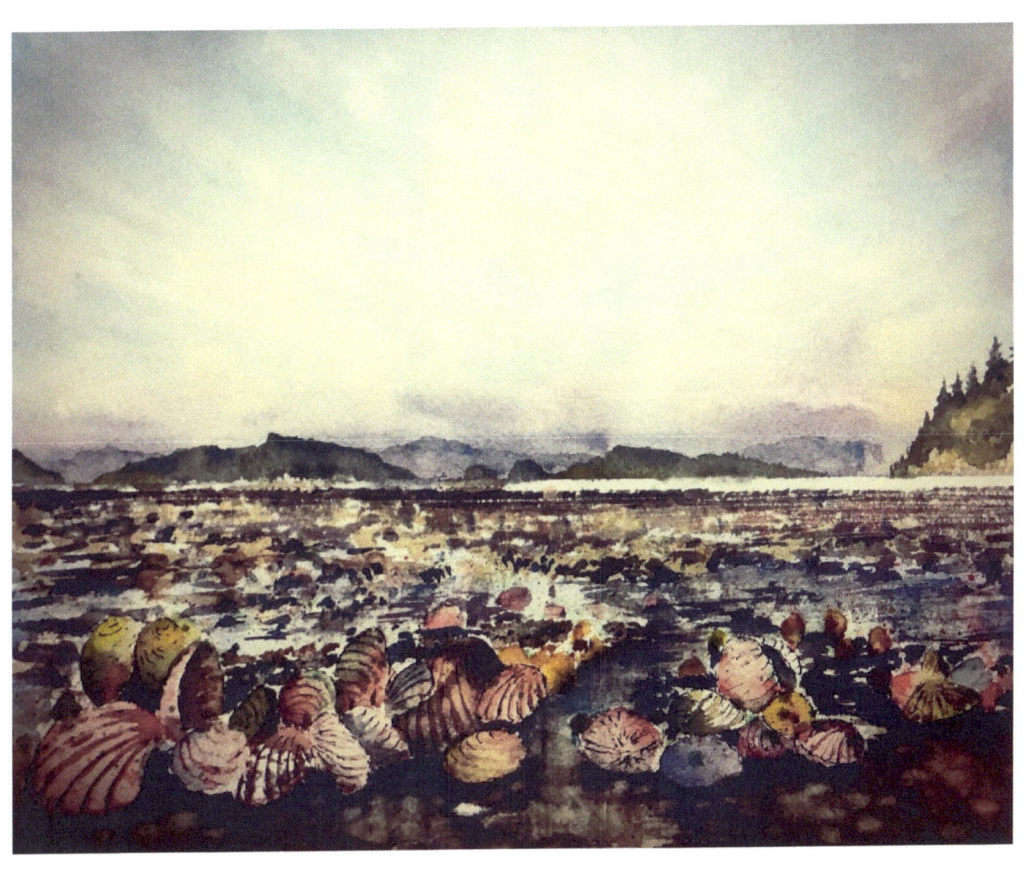

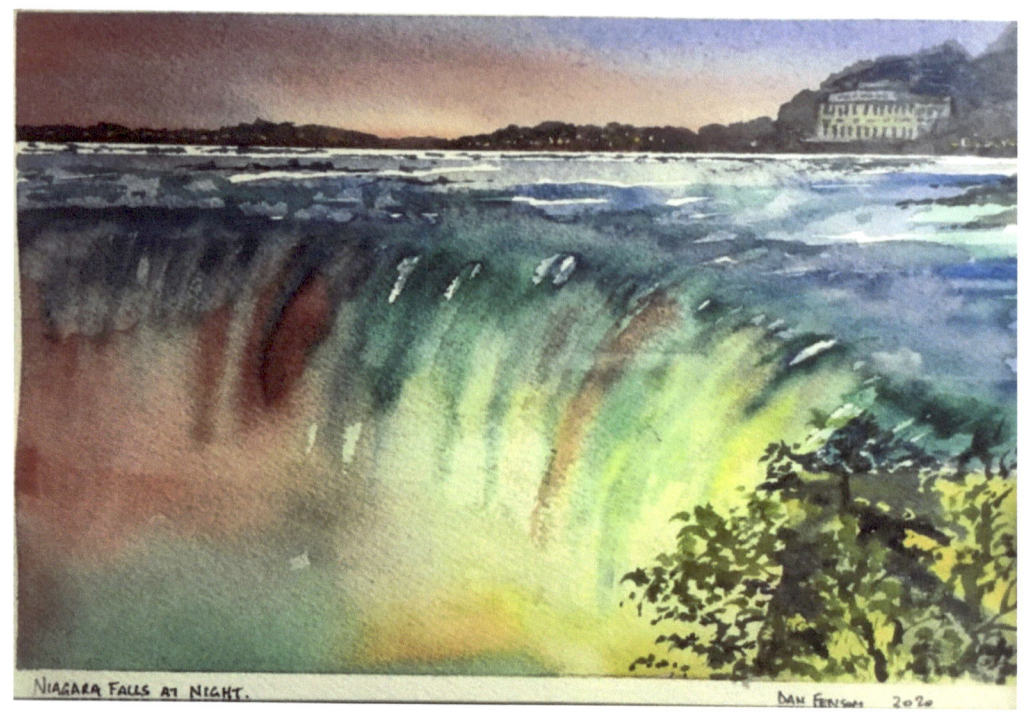

TIME IS TICKING

Time is life

We break in little pieces

Seconds, minutes, hours

Slip right through our fingers

Time never stops

For no man is waiting

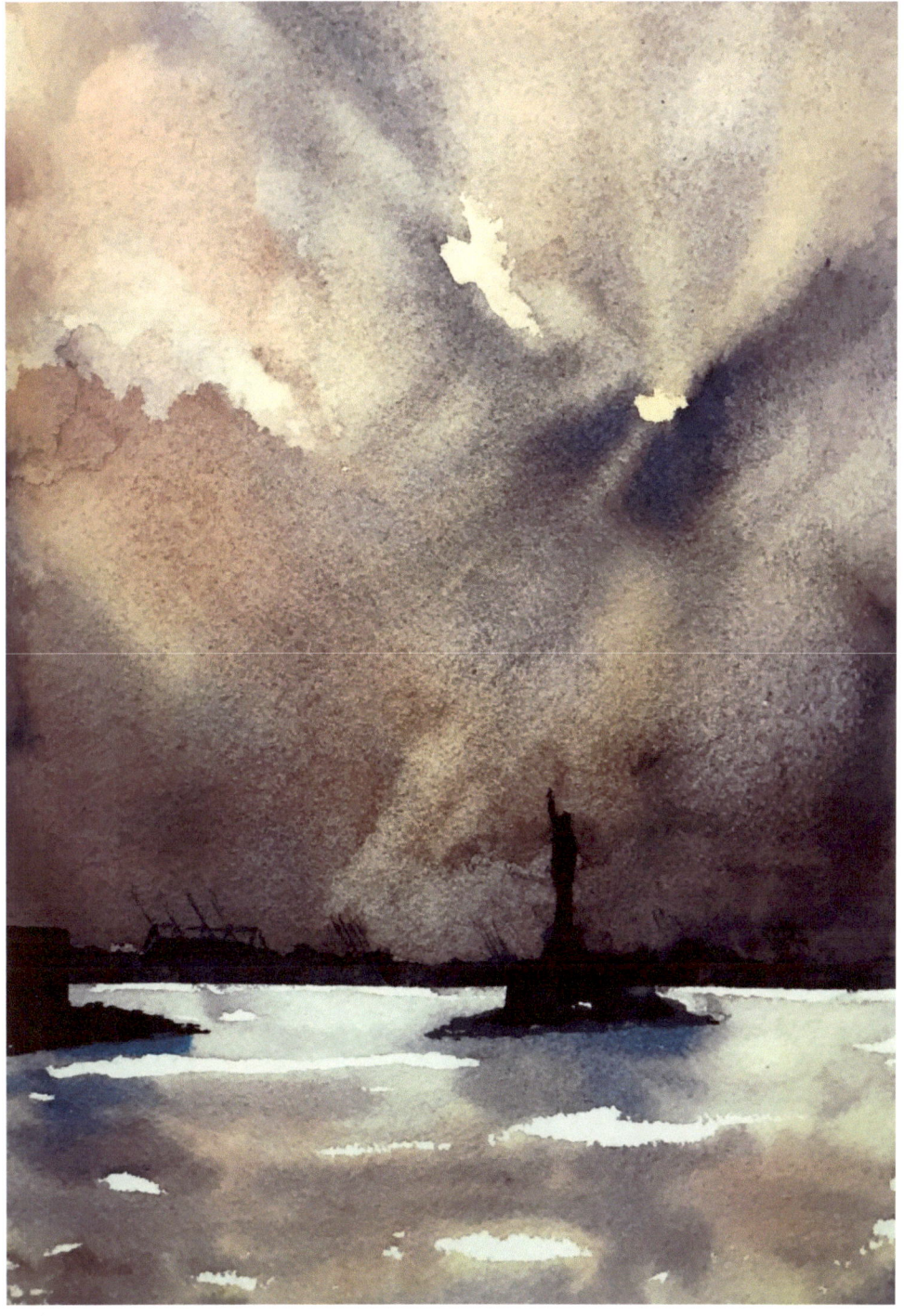

Time passes those

Who spend it hesitating

Time's never owned

It's only ever borrowed

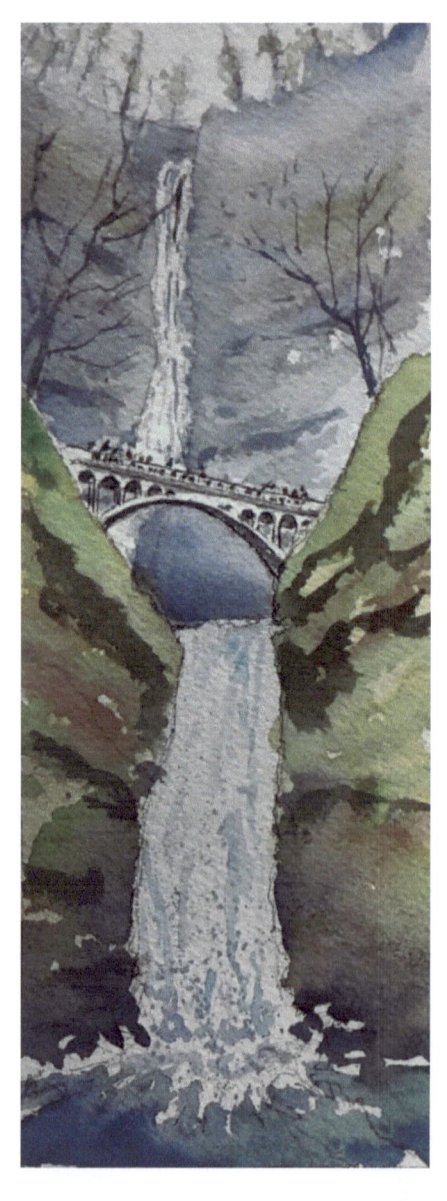

Live each day like

You'll pay the debt tomorrow

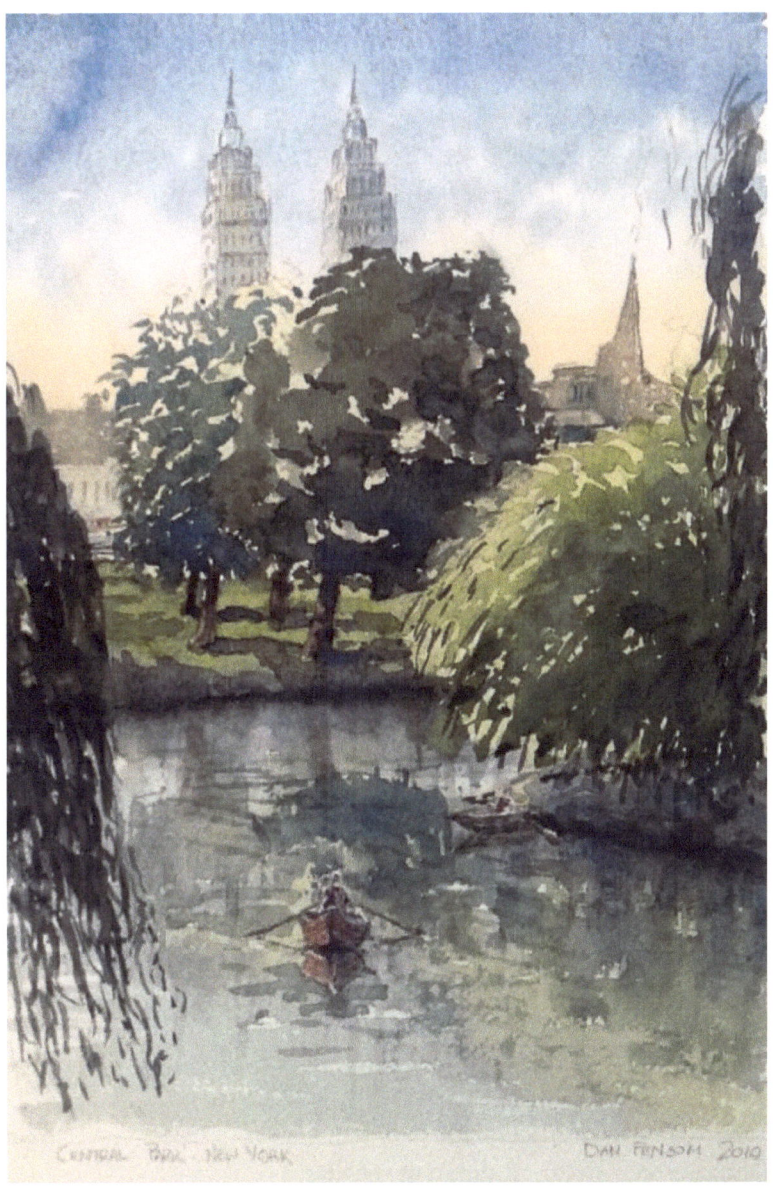

Give your time with love to others,

Give it free and you'll discover

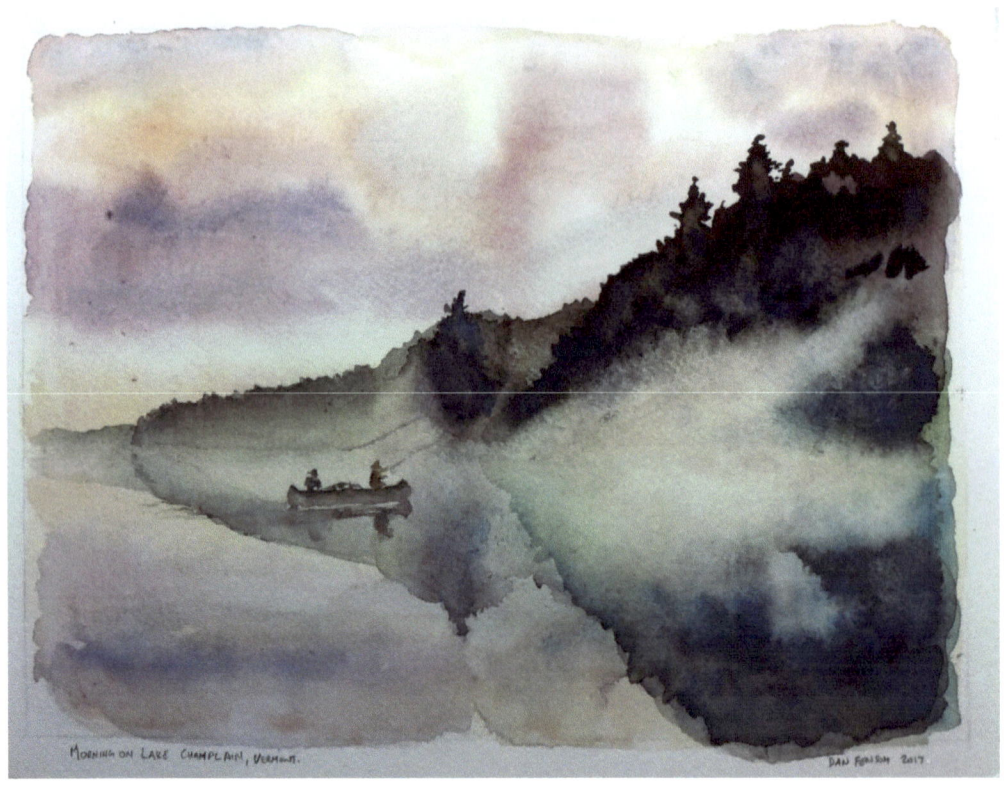

The time you spend will bounce right back

The more you give, the less you lack

Time's a friend to those who grasp

In the future lies the past

Seize the day and you will find

Time to the bold is often kind.

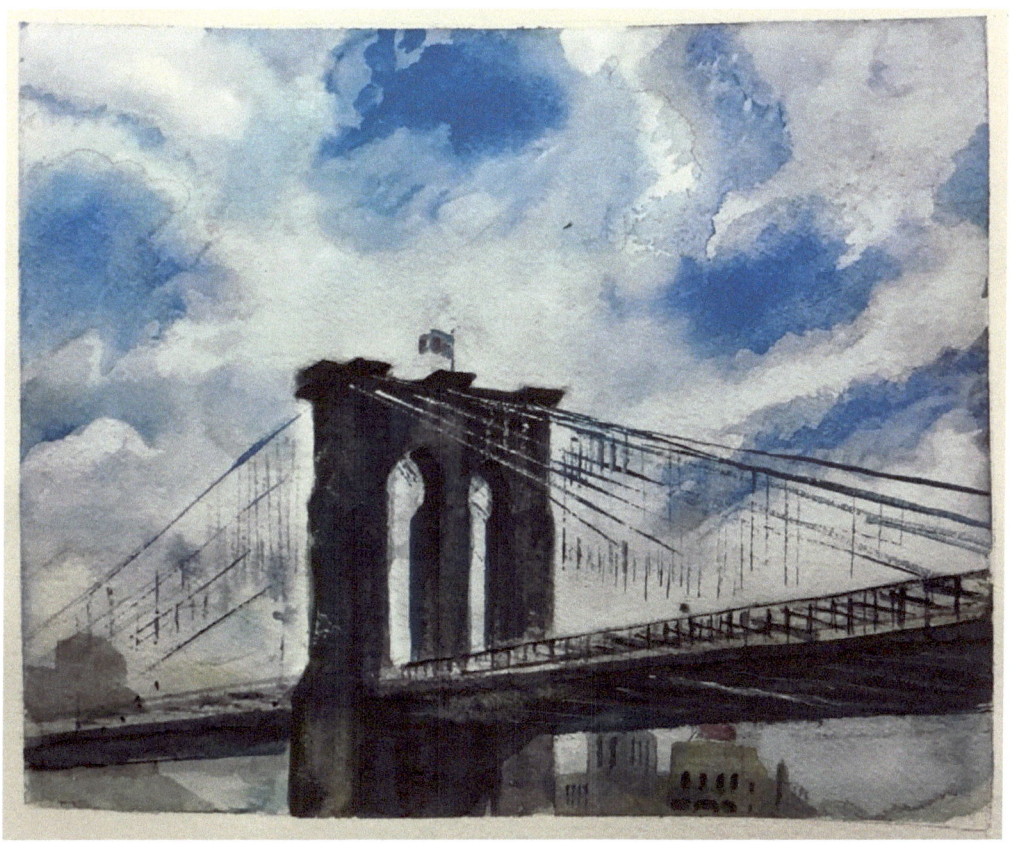

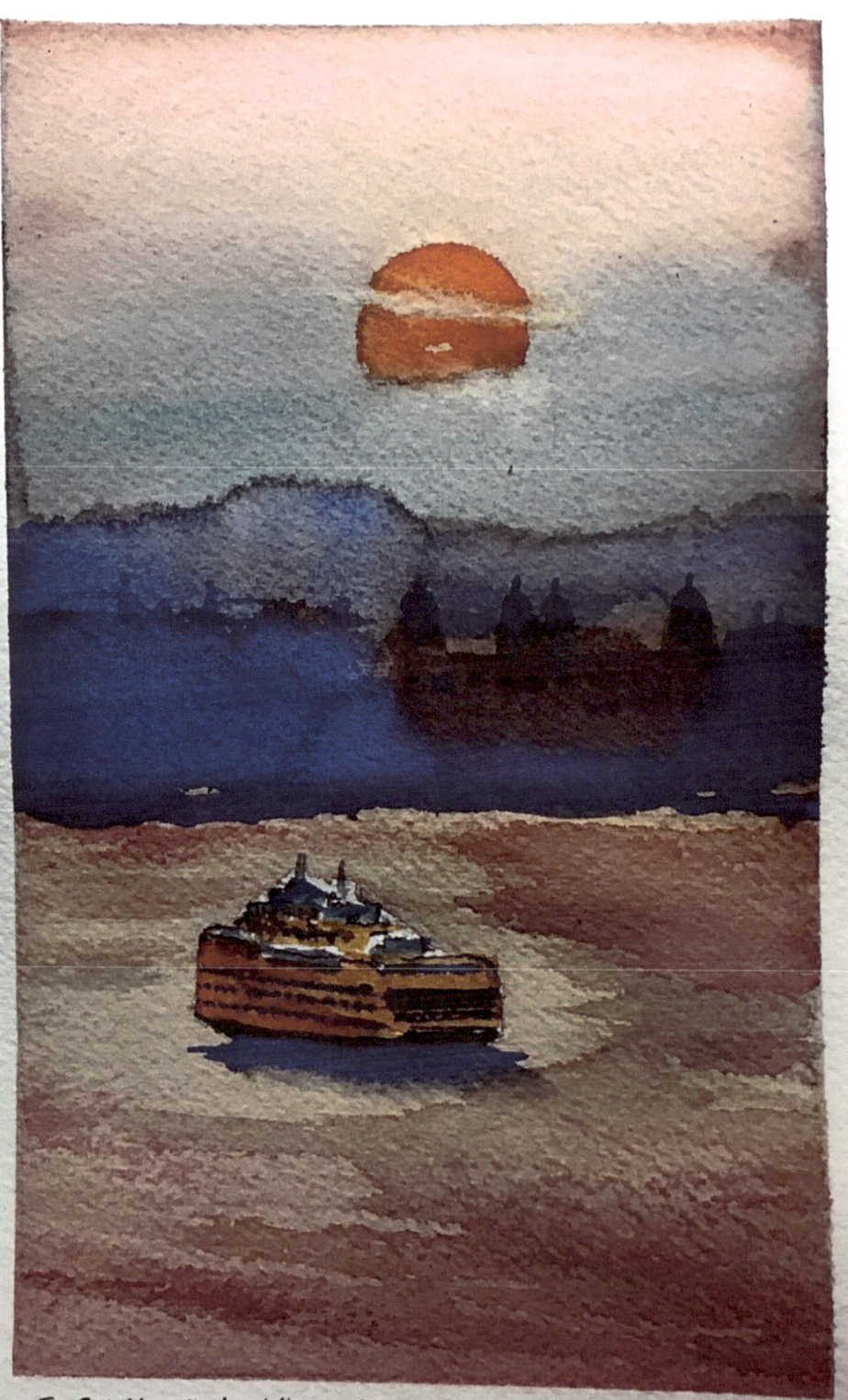

EVENING ON NEW YORK HARBOR — DAN FENSOM 2020

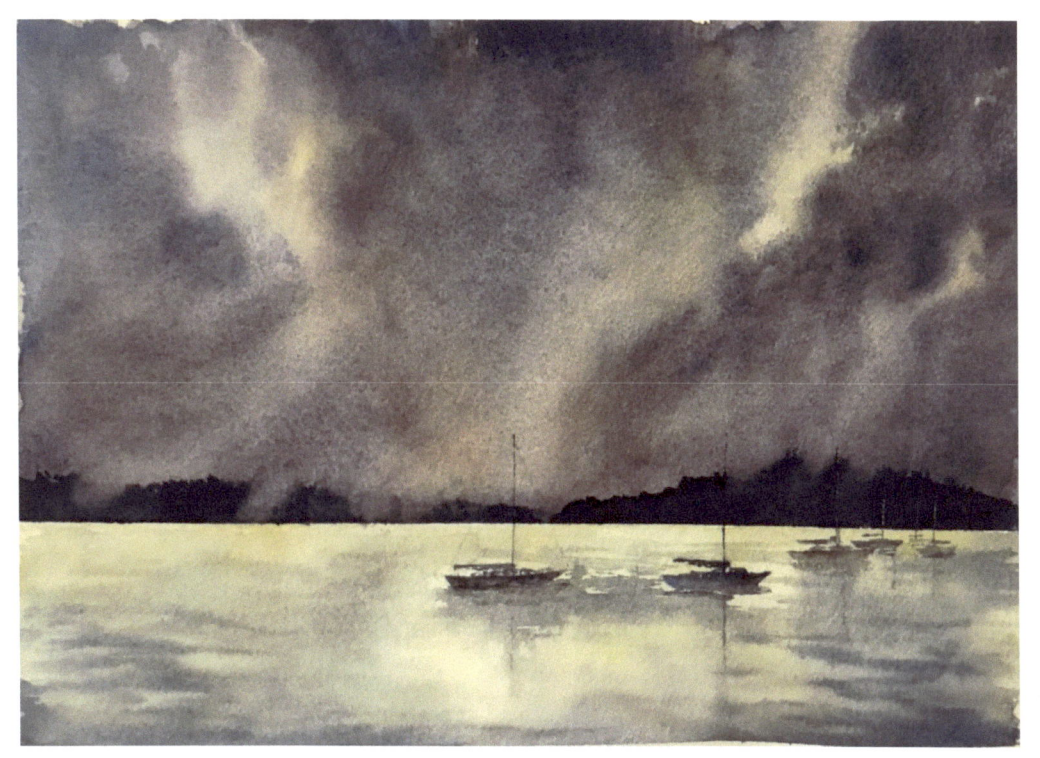

THE CYCLE

Life depends on rivers running

Streams of water ever flowing

Water down a mountain splashing

On the earth it's power crashing

Streams are bouncing, quickly moving

The very earth they're slowly carving

None can stop their ceaseless motion

But rivers end when meeting ocean

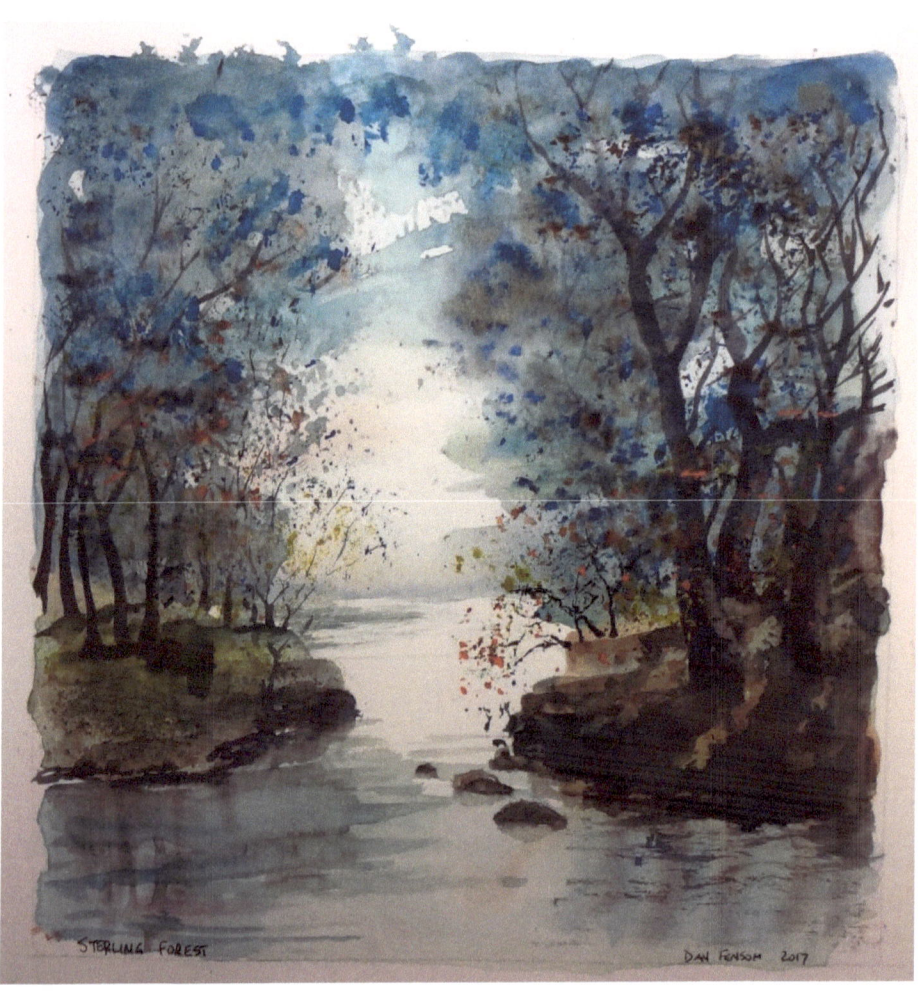

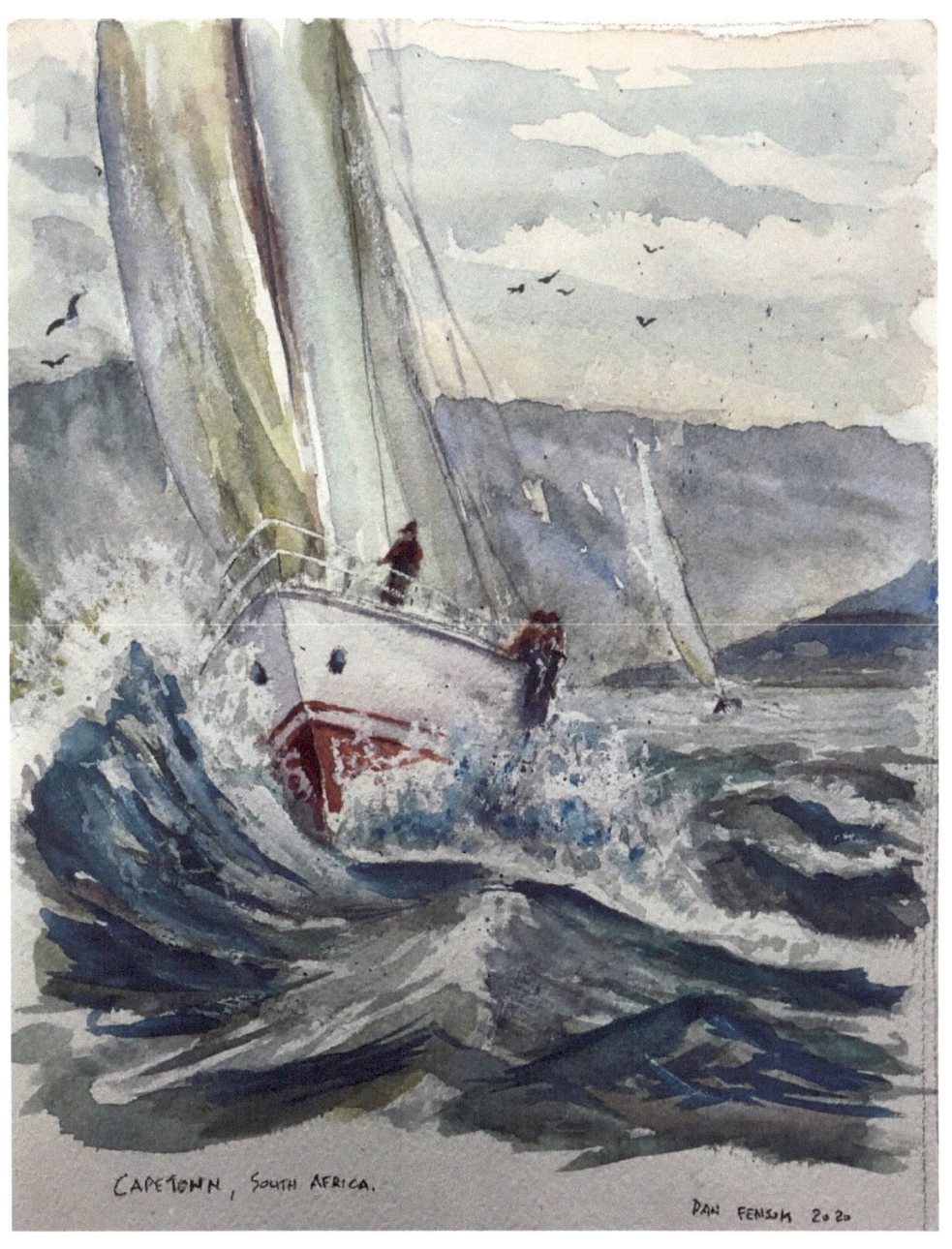

The ocean waves are always racing

The one in front they're always chasing

Rhythmically they rise and fall

The rocky shore awaits them all

Waves don't heed the thunder growing

Don't know about the end they're nearing

But in their sudden crashing ending

Create a mist that is ascending

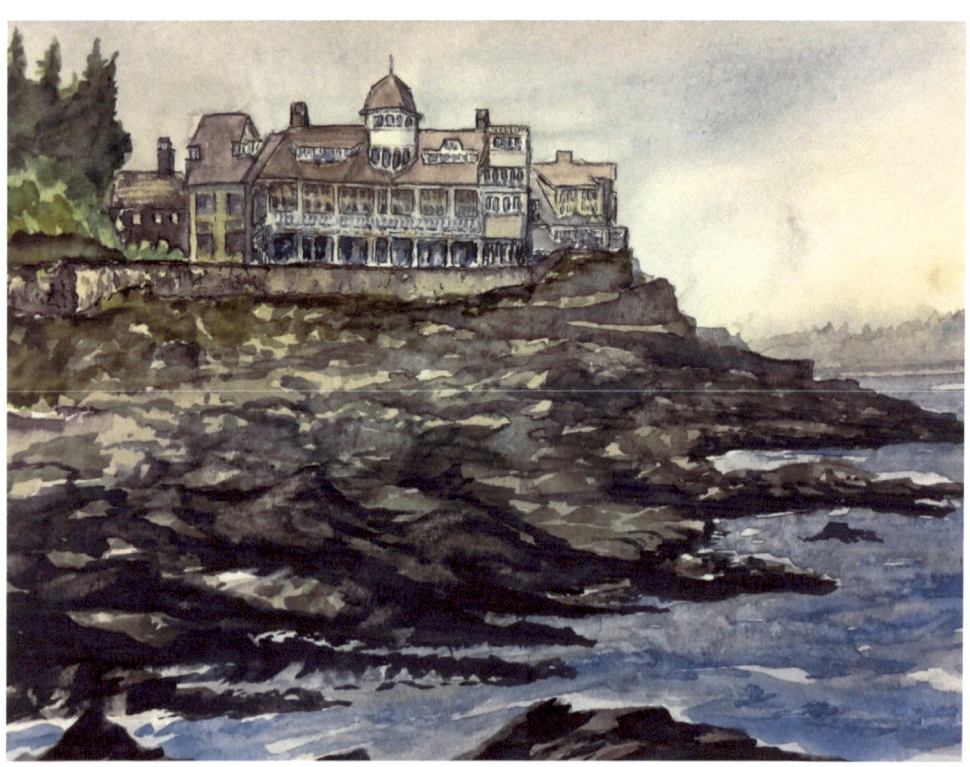

The clouds that rise, slowly forming

To simple molds are not conforming

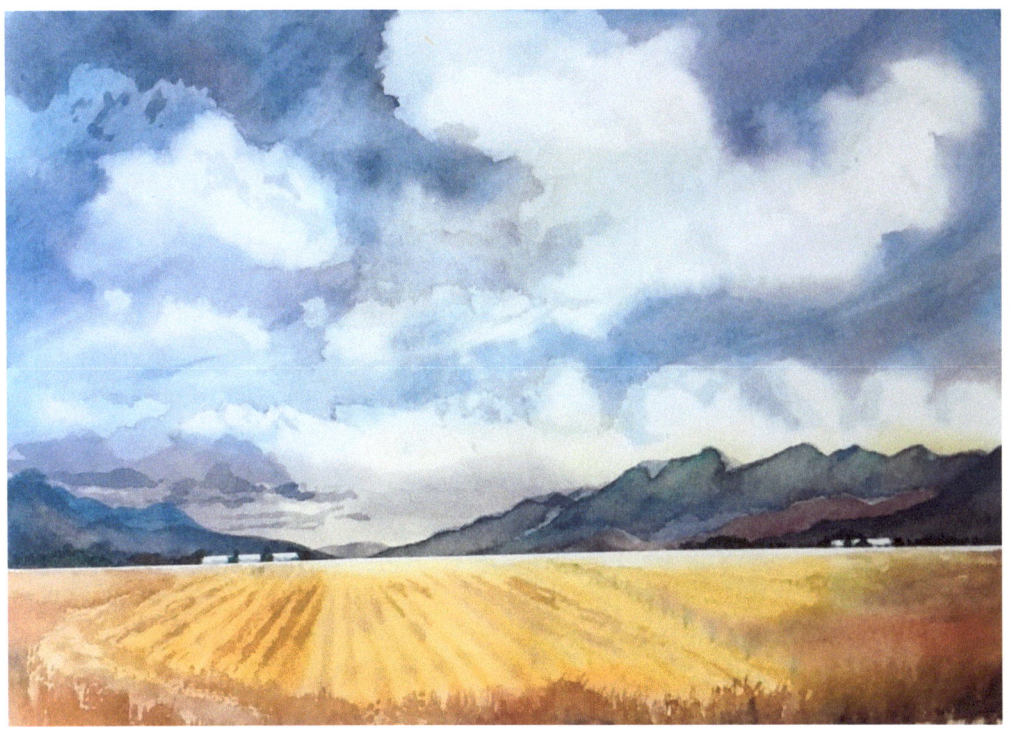

The endless skies they are roaming

Like the birds wind they're roving

But every cloud you see is ending

In sheets of rain they are descending

Until the earth they are soaking

And again the cycle stoking

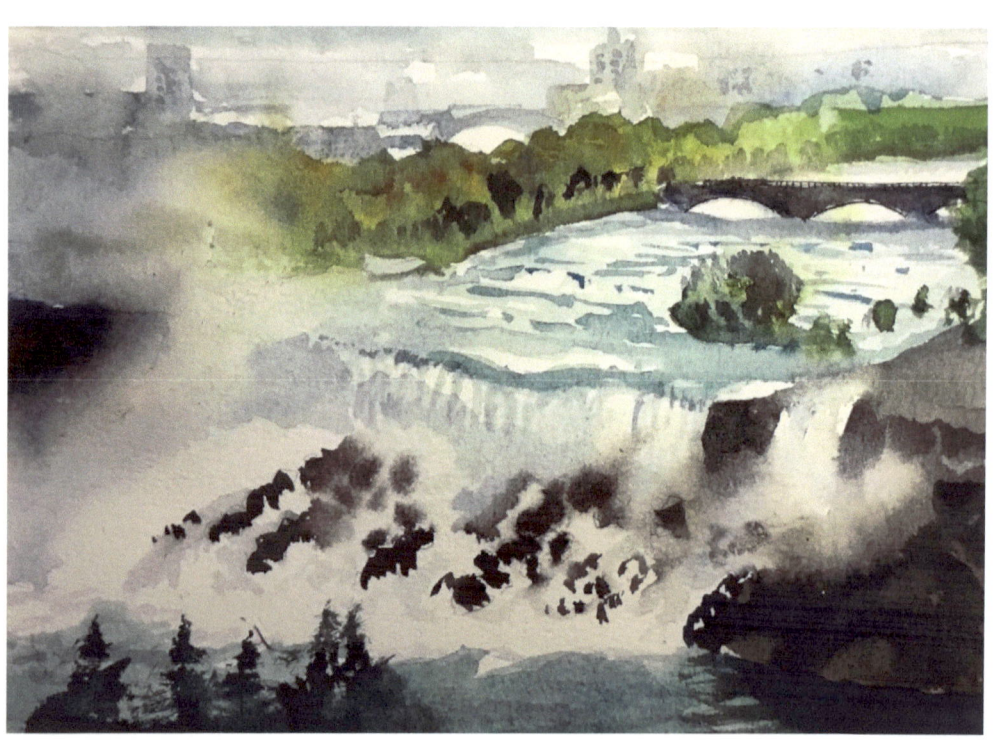

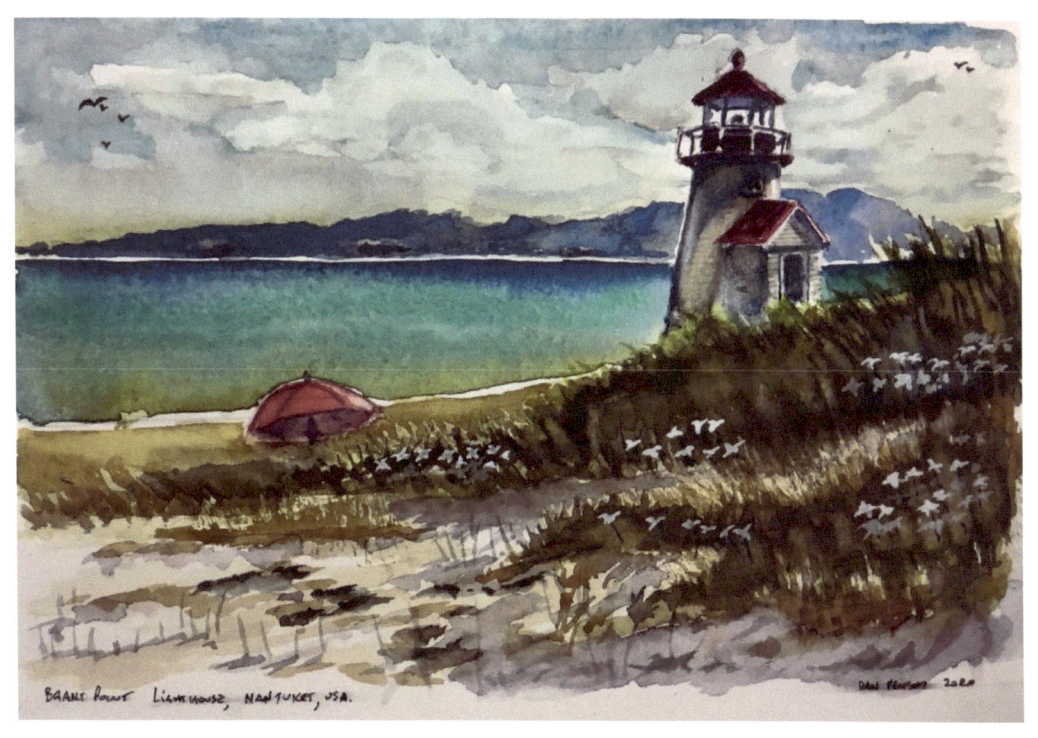

DAYS THAT COUNT

When we're young

Time moves slow

We think it's free

But we don't know

Each day we spend

Costs much more

Than what we spent

The day before

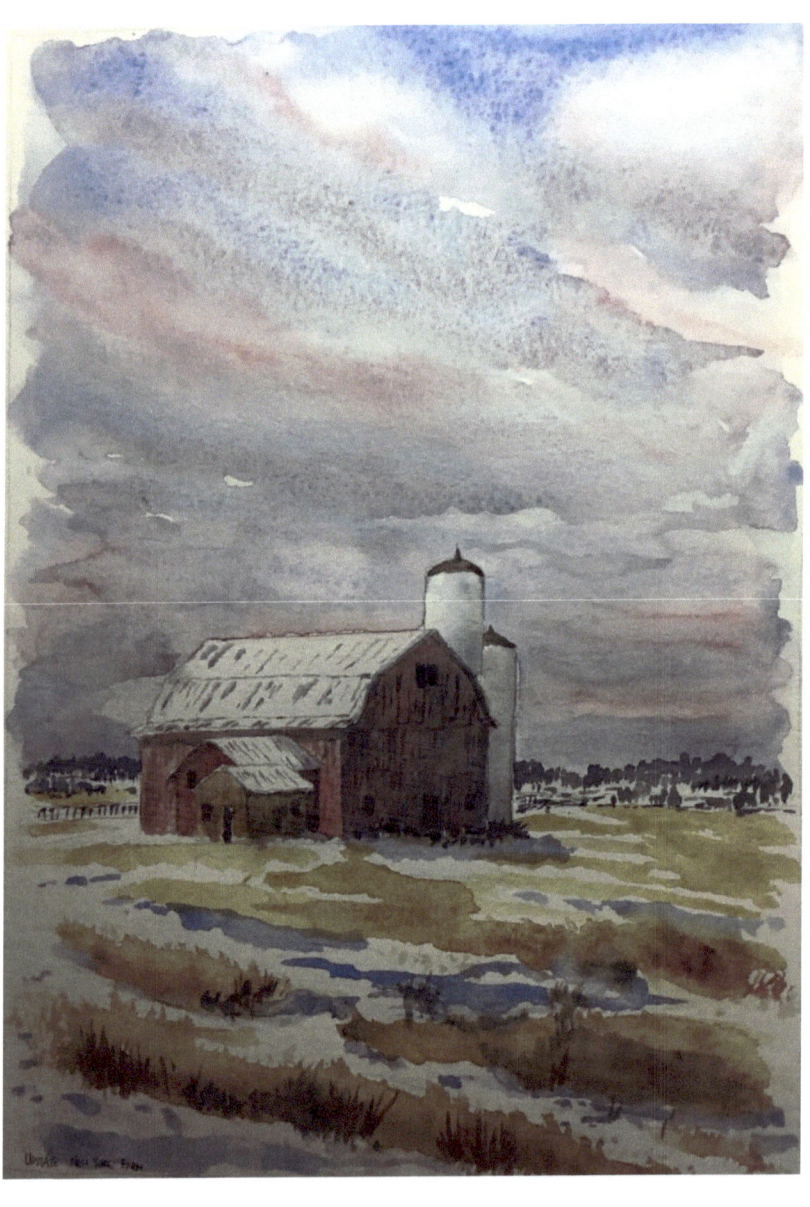

When at last

The last one comes

We'd buy one more

For any sum

You could just live

And each day count

Or…

Live each day

And make it count

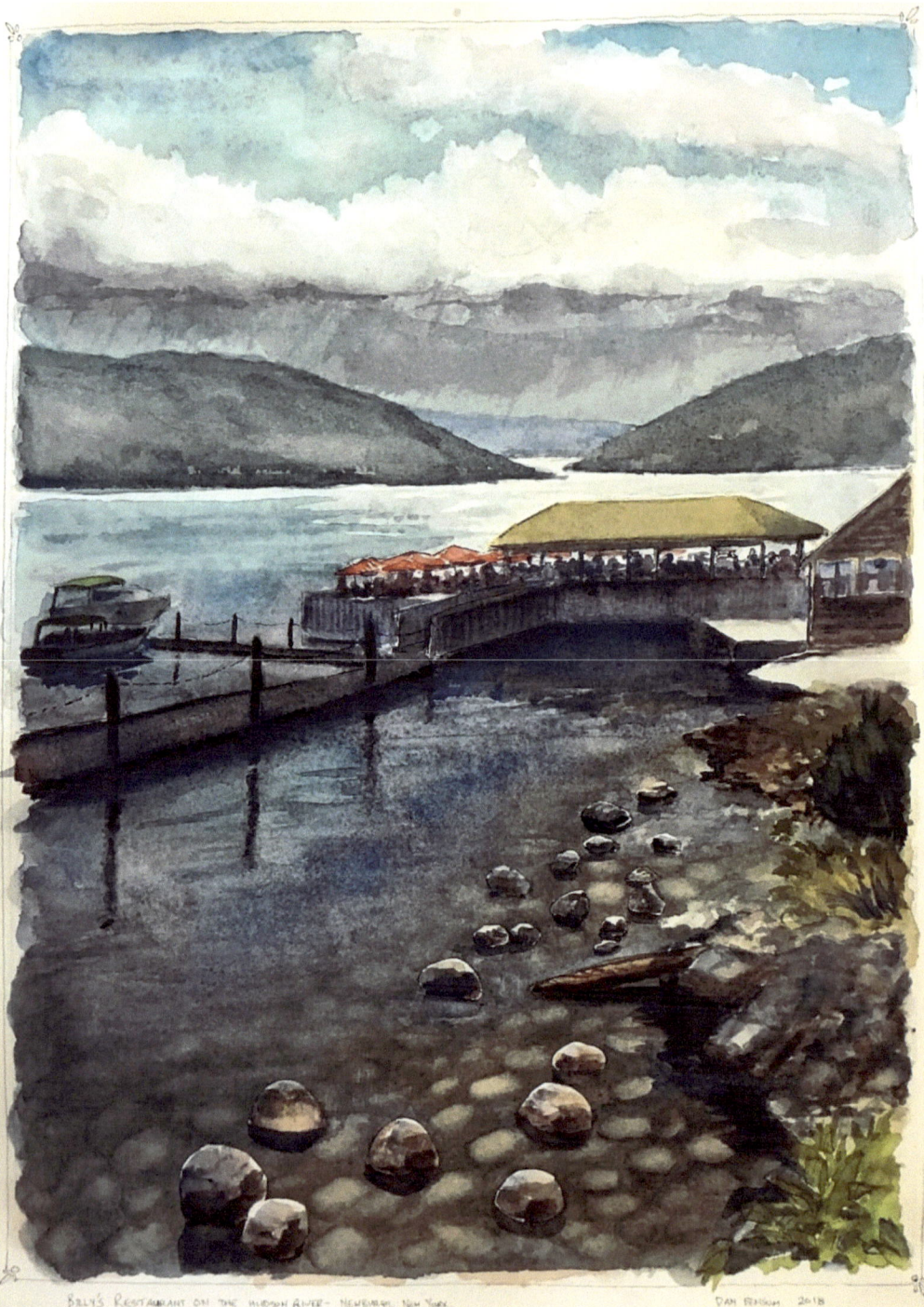

www.ingramcontent.com/pod-product-compliance
Lightning Source LLC
Chambersburg PA
CBHW040331220526
45473CB00009B/2648